Seasonings

Based on the public television series
Hosted by Dede Wilson

Produced by Marjorie Poore Productions
Photography by Alec Fatalevich

Contents

Table of Contents
by Category

Grilled Steak with Shiitake Mushrooms in
    Whole-Grain Mustard Sauce 104

Herb-Marinated Rack of Lamb with Roasted
    Garlic Fingerling Potatoes 141

Linguine Nogada 75

Middle Eastern Beef with Green Beans and
    Potatoes 110

Molasses Baked Chicken 33

One-Wok Curry Chicken 73

Pan-Seared Duck Breasts 76

Polenta Lasagna with Mushrooms Béchamel 127

Potage of Abundance (Beef and Potato Stew) 58

Red Cooking Pork 61

Roasted Goose 27

Vegetarian Fried Rice 69

SWEETS & TREATS

Caramelized Rum-Scented Bananas with
    Bittersweet Chocolate Sauce 143

Chocolate Chiffon Cake 95

Chocolate Fettuccini with Peppered
    Strawberries and Mango 47

Chocolate-Chunk Scones 93

Chocolate-Orange Dream Mousse 128

Cocoa Shortbread Fingers 92

Dark Chocolate Nut Clusters 94

Double Chocolate Sweetheart Cake 80

Espresso Pots de Creme 90

Grilled Fruit and Pound Cake 150

Honey Molasses Peanut Butter Popcorn Balls 19

Italian Meringue Buttercream 133

Marble Two-Chocolate Tart 115

Night Before Christmas Mice 18

Orange Buttermilk Pie 53

Pineapple Iced Cake 34

Queen of Sheba Chocolate Almond Cake 112

Raspberry Almond Cheesecake 77

Snowman Cake 24

Solid Molded Chocolate 118

Stained Glass Butter Cookies 16

Strawberry Sauté 106

Sugarplums 20

Traditional Rolled Sugar Cookies 83

White Cake 131

White Chocolate-Apricot Truffles 117

Breads

Cheese Straws 30

Greek Easter Bread 122

Mushroom Bread 99

Spicy Herbed Bread Sticks 97

Introduction

by Dede Wilson

Welcome to the companion cookbook for *Seasonings with Dede Wilson,* which airs on PBS stations around the country. In every episode we celebrate a special occasion or international holiday with guest expert cookbook authors who specialize in their chosen topic. Here you will find recipes from all our shows, making it possible for you to cook and bake along with us.

Working alongside these chefs and cooks was an incredibly enjoyable and educational experience. Thanksgiving is one of my very favorite holidays and Diane Morgan showed us how to make some colorful and delicious side dishes. We bring you a Kwaanza feast with expert Joyce White featuring recipes from her family—and beans from Louis Armstrong. Master chef Fritz Sonnenschmidt taught us how to make a juicy, flavorful Christmas goose with some of the lightest and tastiest bread dumplings I have ever tried. There were more holiday treats from *Today* show contributor Donata Maggipinto, who created a white winter wonderland right in our studio, and Lauren Chattman, whose cookies kept us all in the holiday spirit. To bring in the New Year, Tom Douglas, Seattle chef extraordinaire, showed us easy ways to feed a crowd with a New Year's Day buffet, delicious enough to be served any time of the year. Jud Simpson, the executive chef for Canada's Parliament, brought us a light and healthy New Year's meal for those of us scaling

back from indulgent holiday eating. For the Chinese New Year, I made dumplings from scratch side-by-side with Grace Young, carefully pleating each wrapper so that they would resemble money and bring prosperity for the coming year.

We celebrated Martin Luther King Jr.'s birthday with Joyce White, who brought us authentic recipes for satisfying and delicious soul food that Dr. King and his family ate at the Ebenezer Baptist Church in Georgia where they worshipped. For Valentine's Day, cookbook author team Bruce Weinstein and Mark Scarbrough prepared a stunning romantic dinner, followed by some ravishing desserts from my friend and expert baker, Rose Levy Beranbaum. Rose also showed me the ins and outs of bread-baking, with some beautiful and fragrant breads. We wrapped up our winter menus with a festive and delicious Mardi Gras celebration brought to us by New Orleans chef Susan Spicer.

Spring kicked off with foods for both Easter and Passover. For Easter, it was an authentic Greek dinner from Canadian cookbook author and TV host Christine Cushing, who prepared a succulent roast lamb and a beautifully braided bread. For some Easter basket fun, *Bon Appetit* contributor Carole Bloom showed us how to make easy chocolate candies. Faye Levy instructed us on the preparation of a proper — and scrumptious — Passover feast, complete with a Mediterranean-flavored stew with green beans, cumin, and tomatoes along with a rich flourless chocolate cake. For Earth Day, Crescent Dragonwagon, a prolific vegetarian author, created a spread with an unforgettable polenta lasagna. Renowned chef and cookbook author Leslie Revsin took us outdoors for a delightful and easy to prepare spring dinner, followed by a Cinco De Mayo celebration with Rafael Palomino, filled with flavorful and creative salsas. For Mother's Day we put ourselves in the talented hands of celebrated Napa Valley chef Maria Helm Sinskey, who prepared a delicious and elegant Mother's Day repast. Our series concluded with cooking pros Pat and Betty from the Reynolds kitchens, who grilled a delicious "no-fuss" meal on the patio to celebrate Memorial Day.

You'll also find some of my favorite recipes for Christmas cookies and a wedding cake. It is my sincere hope that all these recipes will give you a reason to celebrate and cook for your very own holidays and special occasions.

Dede Wilson

THANKSGIVING
SIDES

Cheddar and Jalapeño Corn Bread Stuffing

Diane Morgan/Reprinted from *The Thanksgiving Table* (Chronicle Books)

Serves 12

If you and your guests are real fans of spicy food, dice a couple of fresh jalapeños and sauté them along with the onions and garlic. If you have time, make the corn bread and hard-cook the eggs the day before; assembling the stuffing will seem like a snap.

Vegetable oil cooking spray
8 cups crumbled Cheddar and Jalapeño Corn Bread (recipe follows)
5 cups unseasoned dry bread cubes
3 hard cooked eggs, shelled and chopped
4 tablespoons unsalted butter
Turkey giblets (gizzard, heart, and liver)
1 large yellow onion (about 12 ounces), chopped
2 cloves garlic, minced
1 large green bell pepper, seeded, deribbed, and chopped
3 large ribs celery, chopped
4 large eggs, lightly beaten
1 cup homemade chicken stock or canned low-sodium chicken broth

Preheat oven to 350 degrees F. Coat a deep, 9 by 13-inch baking pan with the cooking spray.

In a very large mixing bowl, combine the corn bread, bread cubes, and chopped eggs.

In a 12-inch sauté pan, melt 2 tablespoons butter over medium heat. Sauté giblets, turning to brown on all sides, until cooked through, about 5 to 7 minutes. Set aside and let cool.

Add 2 tablespoons butter to pan. Sauté onion, garlic, green pepper, and celery until soft and lightly browned, about 5 minutes. Add to bread in the bowl. Finely dice the giblets and add to stuffing mixture. Add beaten eggs and stock and mix well. Put into prepared pan and bake, uncovered, until top is lightly browned and crusty, about 1 hour.

This can bake in the oven with the turkey, or be baked beforehand and reheated when the turkey is out of the oven.

Cheddar and Jalapeño Corn Bread
Vegetable-oil cooking spray
2 cups yellow cornmeal
1 teaspoon salt
1 tablespoon sugar
2 teaspoons baking soda
1½ cups (6 ounces) grated sharp Cheddar cheese
1 can (15 ounces) creamed corn
½ cup canned diced jalapeños, drained
1 cup buttermilk
4 large eggs, lightly beaten
¾ cup (1½ sticks) unsalted butter, melted

Preheat oven to 375 degrees F. Coat a 9 by 13-inch baking pan with cooking spray.

In a large bowl, combine cornmeal, salt, sugar, and baking soda. Add cheese, corn, jalapeños, buttermilk, and eggs, stirring just to blend. Stir in the melted butter. Pour batter into prepared pan, and smooth top with a rubber spatula.

Bake until golden brown and a toothpick comes out clean, about 45 minutes. Let cool in the pan for 15 minutes; then turn out onto a wire rack to cool completely.

Makes one 9 by 13-inch corn bread, enough for 8 cups crumbled, plus extra for snacking.

Praline Sweet Potato Casserole

Diane Morgan/Reprinted from *The Thanksgiving Table* (Chronicle Books)

Serves 8 to 10

Forget about leftovers when it comes to this casserole—there never are any.
Both children and adults will sneak back for seconds, even thirds.

6 large dark-orange fleshed sweet potatoes
  (or yams), about 5½ pounds, scrubbed
¾ cup milk
½ cup (1 stick) unsalted butter
3 large eggs, lightly beaten
¾ cup packed dark brown sugar

Praline topping
4 tablespoons unsalted butter
¾ cup packed dark brown sugar
½ teaspoon salt
½ teaspoon ground cinnamon
½ teaspoon freshly grated nutmeg
¾ cup heavy (whipping) cream
1½ cups pecans, coarsely chopped
2 teaspoons vanilla extract

Preheat oven to 350 degrees F. Pierce each potato several times with a fork and bake in a pan until pierced easily with a fork, 1¼ to 1½ hours. Set aside to cool.

In a small saucepan, heat milk and butter until butter has melted and mixture is hot, but not boiling. Cut cooled potatoes in half, and scoop the flesh into a large bowl, discarding the skins. Use a potato masher, ricer, or food mill to mash the potatoes. Stir in the milk mixture. Whisk in the eggs and continue whisking until well combined. Add brown sugar and stir until thoroughly blended.

Butter a 9 by 13-inch baking pan or an 11-inch round oven-to-table casserole. Spread the sweet potato mixture evenly in the casserole. Set aside while making the topping. Increase oven temperature to 375 degrees F.

To make the praline topping: Melt butter in a 2-quart saucepan over low heat. Stir in brown sugar, salt, cinnamon, nutmeg, cream, and pecans. Heat to a simmer, and cook, stirring constantly, until sugar has dissolved and mixture is thick, about 5 minutes. If it begins to boil and splatter, turn down heat to maintain a simmer. Remove from heat; stir in the vanilla. Pour the topping evenly over the sweet potatoes, spreading it with a rubber spatula.

Bake casserole until the topping is slightly crusty and set, about 30 minutes. Serve immediately.

Succotash of Corn, Chanterelles, Zucchini, and Sweet Red Peppers

Diane Morgan/Reprinted from *The Thanksgiving Table* (Chronicle Books)

Serves 10 to 12

The Narragansett Indians ate a mixture of corn and beans cooked in bear fat.
They called it "misickquatash." Here is an updated version of that dish.

5 fresh ears of corn (see Cook's Notes, below)
3 tablespoons unsalted butter
2 medium zucchini (about 1 pound), cut into
  ½ inch dice
1 large white onion (about 12 ounces), cut into
  ½ inch dice
2 medium red bell peppers, seeded, deribbed,
  and cut into ½ inch dice
1 package (10 ounces) frozen lima beans, thawed
8 ounces fresh chanterelle mushrooms, cleaned,
  trimmed, and quartered (see Cook's Notes)
½ cup minced fresh parsley
Salt and freshly ground pepper

Husk the corn, peel off the silk and discard. Trim the base so you can stand the ear on its end. Using a sharp knife, scrape the kernels from the cob. Discard the cobs.

Bring a large saucepan two-thirds full of water to a boil over high heat. Add corn and simmer for 3 minutes. Drain in a colander, then rinse under cold water until cool. Drain thoroughly, blot to dry, and set aside.

In a 12-inch sauté pan, melt butter over medium-high heat and swirl to coat the pan. Add zucchini and onion dice and sauté, stirring frequently, until just beginning to brown at the edges, about 5 minutes. Add red peppers and sauté 3 minutes longer. Add lima beans, corn kernels, and mushrooms. Sauté, stirring constantly, until mushrooms have softened and the mixture is heated through, about 3 minutes. Stir in parsley, add salt and pepper to taste. Serve immediately, or keep warm for up to 20 minutes.

Cook's Notes: In these days of global markets, fresh corn is available year-round. November corn is probably a hybrid known as Super-sweet, whose higher sugar content makes it caramelize a bit when sautéed, adding richness to the succotash.

Delicate, golden-hued chanterelle mushrooms appear in fall. They are buttery rich in flavor and perfume any dish with a fresh, woodsy scent. If you can't find them fresh, use dried—just soak them in warm water to soften. Or use fresh shiitake or cremini mushrooms.

HOLIDAY COOKIES

Stained Glass Butter Cookies

Lauren Chattman/Reprinted from *Mom's Big Book of Baking* (Harvard Common Press)

Makes about 42 cookies

Melted bits of hard candy in the center of these cookies look like stained glass. For the prettiest cookies, use a fluted cutter. Red and green hard candies are traditional, but butterscotch looks and tastes wonderful also. A sprinkling of sugar adds a sparkly holiday look.

1 cup (2 sticks) unsalted butter, softened
¾ cup sugar
1 large egg yolk
1 teaspoon pure vanilla extract
2¼ cups unbleached all-purpose flour
¾ cup (about 6 ounces) red or green hard candies or butterscotch candies

Using you stand mixer, cream the butter and ½ cup of sugar together in mixing bowl on medium-high until fluffy. Add the egg yolk and vanilla and beat until incorporated, scraping down the sides of the bowl. Add the flour and mix on low until the dough comes together in a ball.

Divide into 3 equal balls. Wrap each in plastic wrap and refrigerate for at least 2 hours and up to 2 days. (The dough can be frozen for up to 1 month; defrost it in the refrigerator before use.)

Preheat the oven to 375 degrees F. Line a large baking sheet with parchment paper.

Use a food processor fitted with a metal blade to process the candies until they are finely ground, and put aside in a small bowl. If you are using more than one color of candy, process each separately.

Remove 1 ball of dough from refrigerator and knead 4 or 5 times on a lightly floured work surface to soften. With a lightly floured rolling pin, roll out to ⅛ inch thick. Using a small glass or biscuit cutter, cut into 3-inch circles. Using small cookie cutters or a sharp paring knife, make decorative cuts in the center of each cookie, leaving a cutout area to fill with candy. Transfer cookies to prepared baking sheet. Using a very small measuring spoon, carefully fill each cutout with candy, and sprinkle with some of the ¼ cup sugar. Refrigerate the scraps.

Bake until they are firm and golden around the edges, about 8 minutes. Let them cool completely on the baking sheet. Repeat with the remaining dough balls and then the chilled scraps, using fresh parchment paper.

These will keep in an airtight container for several days.

Night Before Christmas Mice

Dede Wilson/ Reprinted from *A Baker's Field Guide to Christmas Cookies* (Harvard Common Press)

Makes 40 mice

These beguiling little sugar cookie mice, with their chocolate eyes and noses, almond ears, and licorice tails, delight all who see them perched on the edge of a cookie plate.

Cookies
3 cups all-purpose flour
¼ teaspoon salt
1 cup (2 sticks) unsalted butter, at room temperature, cut into tablespoon-sized pieces
¾ cup sugar
1 teaspoon almond or vanilla extract
1 large egg
Sliced natural almonds

Decoration
10 feet red or black licorice laces (thin, spaghetti-like strands), cut into 3-inch lengths
6 ounces semisweet chocolate, melted

Preheat oven to 350 degrees F. Line two cookie sheet pans with parchment paper.

Whisk flour and salt together in a small bowl to aerate and combine; set aside.

Place butter in mixer bowl and beat with flat paddle on medium-high speed until creamy, about 2 minutes. Add sugar gradually and continue beating until light and fluffy, about 3 minutes, scraping down the bowl once or twice; beat in almond or vanilla extract. Beat in egg.

Turn mixer off, add about a third of the flour mixture, and turn machine on at low speed. Gradually add remaining flour, mixing just until blended, scraping down bowl once or twice. Scrape dough onto large piece of plastic wrap and wrap completely. Refrigerate at least 2 hours or until firm enough to roll. Dough may be refrigerated overnight. (You may freeze dough up to 1 month double-wrapped in plastic wrap; defrost in refrigerator overnight before proceeding.)

Roll dough between your palms into 1¼-inch ovals. Slightly elongate one end to form nose. Gently pinch the bridge of the nose to form eye sockets. Place two sliced almonds behind eyes to make ears. Place mice on prepared cookie sheet 2 inches apart.

Bake for 15 minutes or until light golden brown on the bottoms and around the edges. Place pans on racks and immediately insert skewer about ½ inch into each mouse's rounded posterior. Remove skewer and insert 3-inch length of licorice for tail; it will wedge in and adhere to the still-warm cookie. Place melted chocolate in parchment cone and snip tiny opening. Pipe small chocolate eyes and nose in appropriate places. Place pan in refrigerator until chocolate has firmed up. Cookies may be stored at room temperature in an airtight container, in a single layer, for up to 2 weeks.

Honey Molasses Peanut Butter Popcorn Balls

Dede Wilson/ Reprinted from *A Baker's Field Guide to Christmas Cookies* (Harvard Common Press)

Makes 18 popcorn balls

*These sweet, easy-to-make treats would be welcomed at any holiday party—
and you can tie ribbons around them and hang them as decorations.*

12 cups popped popcorn
¼ cup honey
¼ cup unsulphured molasses
**¼ cup natural non-hydrogenated salted
    peanut butter**
1 cup sugar
**12 yards ¼-inch ribbon, cut into 24-inch pieces
    (optional, for hanging)**

Put popped popcorn in a large mixing bowl. Whisk together honey, molasses, and peanut butter in a small saucepan until smooth. Stir in sugar; place over high heat and bring to a boil, swirling the pan a few times to help the mixture blend. Cook until mixture reaches 260 degrees F. (If you are not using a candy thermometer, here's your guideline: if you drip the mixture into a glass of cold water, it will form a hard ball.) Remove from heat and immediately pour over the popcorn. Quickly stir the mixture to thoroughly coat the corn before the syrup hardens too much; it should still be warm to the touch.

Scoop up a handful (about ½ cup, but you can do this by eye) and compress into a ball about 2 inches across. Set on rack to cool. If desired, tie a ribbon around each ball with center of ribbon on center bottom of ball, knot at the top (there will be two long ends), and knot ends together. You will have a large loop for slipping over tree boughs. Balls may be stored at room temperature in an airtight container for up to 4 days.

Sugarplums

Dede Wilson/ Reprinted from *A Baker's Field Guide to Christmas Cookies* (Harvard Common Press)

Makes 36 sugarplums

These small candies made from a melange of dried fruit are great to make with kids, in which case use the orange juice. For adults, try the "spirited" variation.

Sugarplums

½ cup finely chopped pecans
¼ cup finely chopped dates
¼ cup finely chopped dried figs
¼ cup finely chopped dried plums (prunes)
¼ cup finely chopped dried cherries
¼ cup finely chopped golden raisins
¼ cup unsweetened grated coconut
2 tablespoons rum, orange liqueur, or orange juice

Optional Toppings

Powdered or granulated sugar
Finely chopped almonds, hazelnuts, pecans,
    pistachios, or walnuts
Finely grated bittersweet chocolate
Cocoa powder
Unsweetened grated coconut

The key to this recipe is to have the nuts and fruits all the same small size. Chop them by hand, or chop one by one in a food processor fitted with metal blade, pulsing on and off until the desired size is reached.

Place nuts, all the dried fruit, coconut, and liquid of choice in medium bowl. Mix together by hand until thoroughly combined; the mixture should hold together when compressed. If it is too dry, add a little more liquid.

Roll mixture into 1-inch balls, compressing so it sticks together. Place sugar in small bowl and roll sugarplums in it to coat completely; place in small fluted cups if desired.

For the optional toppings: instead of sugar, roll the sugarplums in a small bowl of any of the suggested toppings. Try a few different versions, such as some rolled in pistachios, others in cocoa or coconut for a real variety of flavors, colors, and textures. Sugarplums may be refrigerated in an airtight container for up to one month.

WHITE WINTER WONDERLAND

Shellfish Gratins

Donata Maggipinto/Reprinted from *Christmas Family Gatherings* (Chronicle Books)

Serves 6

Feel free to vary the shellfish selection, or use only one type. If you don't have individual dishes, simply spoon the cooked mixture into a 1½-quart oval gratin baking dish and proceed as directed, increasing the total baking time to about 15 minutes, or until heated through.

**4 tablespoons (½ stick) unsalted butter, plus
¾ cup (1½ sticks) cut into small pieces**
1 small yellow onion, finely chopped
1½ cups finely chopped mushrooms
¼ cup all-purpose flour
1½ cups half and half
½ cup dry sherry
2 teaspoons dry mustard
4 egg yolks
Salt and freshly ground pepper
**½ pound crabmeat, picked over well to remove
any bits of shell**
½ pound small shrimp, peeled and deveined
**½ pound lobster meat, picked over to remove
any bits of shell**
1½ cups fresh bread crumbs
Lemon wedges

Preheat the oven to 400 degrees F.

In a saucepan over medium heat, melt 4 tablespoons butter. When it begins to foam, add onion and mushrooms and cook until onion is translucent, about 5 minutes. Add the flour and cool, stirring, for 3 minutes. Add the half and half, sherry, and dry mustard and cook, stirring constantly, until mixture thickens and is smooth, about 8 minutes.

Put the egg yolks in a small bowl and stir about ¼ cup of the sauce into them. Add the salt and pepper to taste and pour mixture back into the pan, mixing thoroughly. Do not let the mixture boil (reduce the heat if necessary).

Add all the shellfish and heat until warmed through. Divide the mixture evenly among six ¾-cup gratin dishes or ramekins. Top with the bread crumbs and dot with the ¾ cup butter. Bake the gratins until the shellfish is hot and the crumbs are brown, 5 to 10 minutes. Serve immediately, accompanied with lemon wedges.

Roasted Goose

Fritz Sonnenschmidt

Serves 6 to 8

Roast Goose is a traditional and popular Christmas main dish in Europe. Larger than a duck, it has wonderful flavor that gives a hint of beef, turkey, and chicken all in one. You can purchase goose either fresh or frozen.

1 young goose (10 pounds)
2 tablespoons loose black tea
1½ cups apple, peeled, cored, and quartered
1 cup peeled onions, quartered
1 teaspoon sage
⅓ cup diced carrots
⅓ cup diced onions
⅓ cup diced celery
2 cups boiling water
4 cups chicken stock
String for trussing bird

Preheat oven to 400 degrees F.

Rinse goose and pat dry inside and out. Season with salt and pepper, and rub with tea leaves.

In a medium bowl, mix together apples, onions, and sage, and fill cavity with this stuffing. Truss goose, rub with salt and pepper and place in oiled roasting pan. Add diced carrots, onions, and celery and boiling water to the pan. Place into a preheated oven. When liquid has evaporated, reset oven heat to 350 degrees and roast, basting often with the goose drippings, for 2 to 2 ½ hours. Remove goose from oven and let rest for 10 minutes. Transfer goose to a platter, remove string, and surround with apple-onion stuffing. Meanwhile, prepare sauce by adding chicken stock to browned vegetable mixture in the roasting pan. Deglaze and simmer for 10 to 15 minutes. Using an immersion or regular blender, purée mixture until smooth. Adjust seasoning to taste.

Bread Dumplings

Fritz Sonnenschmidt

Serves 4 to 6

Here's a wonderful accompaniment for roast goose or any roasted meat or poultry.
They plump up beautifully in the boiling water, producing tender, succulent results. Remember to
keep your hands moist while forming the dumplings.

4 cups unseasoned bread croutons
2 cups hot milk
2 tablespoons butter
3 tablespoons chopped onions
1 tablespoon chopped parsley
½ teaspoon baking powder
3 tablespoons flour
⅓ teaspoon nutmeg
1 teaspoon salt
4 eggs, beaten
Unseasoned bread crumbs (optional)

In a medium bowl, pour 1½ cups hot milk over croutons and let sit for 5 minutes. (Add more milk if mixture is too dry.) Heat butter in a sauté pan and sauté chopped onions until lightly brown. Add chopped parsley during the last minute.

Pour sautéed mixture over soaked bread croutons. In another bowl, combine flour, baking powder, salt, and nutmeg. Add this to the bread mixture and mix well. Add beaten eggs and mix again. Let mixture rest for 45 minutes at room temperature. If mixture is too soft, add some unseasoned bread crumbs.

While mixture is resting, fill a 5-quart stock or soup pot about two-thirds full with water, add 2 teaspoons kosher salt, and bring to a boil. After bread mixture has rested, wet your hands to keep mixture from sticking, and shape round dumplings approximately 1½ to 2 inches in diameter. Drop dumplings into boiling water, turn heat down to a simmer, cover the pot and let simmer for 20 minutes. Remove with a slotted spoon and serve as a hot side dish.

CELEBRATE
KWAANZA

Cheese Straws

Joyce White/Reprinted from *Soul Food: Recipes and Reflections from African American Kitchens* (HarperCollins Publishers)

Makes about 4 dozen

These crisp, light, and cheesy breadsticks are real crowd pleasers.
Try placing them in a vase for a striking table centerpiece.

8 tablespoons (1 stick) butter or margarine, softened
3 cups finely grated extra sharp Cheddar cheese
2 cups all-purpose flour
¼ teaspoon salt
½ cup cold milk or light cream
1 egg white, lightly beaten
Paprika
Sesame seeds

In a large bowl combine the butter or margarine and the cheese. Using fingertips, blend them together until well mixed.

Sift in the flour and salt, and, still using your fingers, blend in the flour with the cheese and butter mixture until it resembles tiny peas or very coarse cornmeal.

Sprinkle the cold milk or cream over this, a tablespoon at a time, using a fork to lift up the dough so that all portions are moistened.

Quickly form the dough into a ball, squeezing firmly to make it hold a shape.

Wrap the dough in plastic wrap, wax paper, or aluminum foil and chill for 15 minutes.

Preheat the oven to 400 degrees F. Scatter the work surface lightly with flour. Divide the dough in half.

Roll out half of the dough into a 10 by 10-inch square. Using a sharp knife, cut it into strips about 5 inches long and ½ inch wide.

Twist each strip like a candy stick and pinch each end. Brush the tops with a little of the beaten egg white and sprinkle generously with paprika or sesame seeds.

Roll out the remaining half of the dough, and cut and shape in the same way.

Place the cheese straws on a large ungreased baking dish. (You may need to bake two batches.) Set the pan on the lower shelf of the hot oven and bake for 8 to 10 minutes, or until golden brown and crisp, turning over at least once during the baking.

Louisiana Red Beans

Joyce White/Reprinted from *Soul Food: Recipes and Reflections from African American Kitchens*
(HarperCollins Publishers)

Serves 8

The purpose of soaking the beans is to remove some of the gas-causing sugars in dried legumes. It also softens the skin which reduces the cooking time. Be sure not to skip this very important step.

1 pound dried small red beans, soaked
1 onion
1 green pepper
8 cloves garlic
2 tablespoons vegetable oil
¼ cup chopped parsley
5 to 6 cups water
½ teaspoon freshly ground black pepper
1 bay leaf
½ pound smoked ham, preferably with bone
1 teaspoon salt

Rinse the soaked beans well with cold water and set aside. Slice the onion, core and dice the green pepper, and mince the garlic.

Heat the oil in a large heavy pot. Add the onion, green pepper, garlic, and parsley. Sauté over low heat for 4 or 5 minutes. Add 5 cups of water, soaked beans, black pepper, bay leaf, and ham. Bring to a boil. Reduce the heat to simmer, cover, and cook for 1½ to 2 hours, stirring occasionally, or until the beans are tender and creamy. (If the beans become too dry, heat the remaining 1 cup of water and add as needed.)

When the beans are tender, remove a cup or so from the pot, place in a bowl and mash with a fork. Stir the mashed beans back into the pot.

Remove the ham from the pot, cut the meat into small pieces and stir back into the pot. Discard the bone.

Stir in the salt, if needed, and simmer the beans for 15 minutes more. Serve the beans over hot rice.

Molasses Baked Chicken

Joyce White/Reprinted from *Soul Food: Recipes and Reflections from African American Kitchens* (HarperCollins Publishers)

Serves 4

Here's a quick chicken dish with plenty of spice, tang, and sweetness.
The molasses gives the chicken a beautifully golden, crisp crust.

1 chicken, 3¼ to 3½ pounds
1 teaspoon salt
Black pepper, to taste
½ to 1 teaspoon allspice or cinnamon
2 tablespoons cider vinegar
2 tablespoons dark molasses or dark syrup
2 tablespoons spicy brown mustard

Preheat the oven to 400 degrees F.

Cut the chicken into serving pieces: the breast into halves, the legs and thighs separated, plus the wings, for a total of 8 pieces. Trim off any visible fat.

Rinse the chicken pieces under running water, drain, and pat dry with paper towels. Sprinkle the chicken with the salt, black pepper, and allspice or cinnamon.

In a small bowl combine the vinegar, molasses or dark syrup, and mustard. Mix well with a fork or wire whisk.

Coat the chicken with the mixture, rubbing well into the skin and flesh.

Lightly oil a large roasting pan, and place the chicken in it. Set the pan on the lower rack of the hot oven and bake for 20 minutes or until the pieces are golden brown.

Using long-handled tongs, turn pieces over and bake for 20 minutes longer. Chicken is done when the pieces are glazed and golden and the juices run clear when meat is pierced with a knife.

Pineapple Iced Cake

Joyce White/Reprinted from *Brown Sugar* (HarperCollins Publishers)

Serves 12 to 14

The secret to this scrumptious dessert lies in the irresistibly creamy filling, which also serves as the icing. This is a special occasion cake that will be sure to leave lasting impressions.

Cake Layers
3 cups cake flour
2½ teaspoons baking powder
½ teaspoon baking soda
¼ teaspoon salt
½ pound (2 sticks, 1 cup) unsalted butter, softened
1½ cups granulated sugar
4 large eggs, at room temperature
1½ teaspoons vanilla extract
1 cup buttermilk, at room temperature.
Softened butter (or grease) and flour for cake pans

Preheat oven to 350 degrees F. Butter three 8-inch cake pans, dust with flour and shake out excess.

Sift the flour with the baking powder, baking soda, and salt, and set aside.

Combine the butter and sugar in the bowl of a standing mixer fitted with the paddle attachment, or use a large mixing bowl and a handheld electric mixer. Beat the mixture on medium-high or creaming speed for 3 to 5 minutes or until light and fluffy, scraping the bowl once or twice with a rubber spatula. Beat in the eggs one at a time, beating about 30 seconds after each addition and scraping the bowl as needed. Stir in the vanilla extract.

Alternately add portions of flour and buttermilk to the creamed mixture, mixing on low speed only until blended after each addition, ending with flour. Then beat the batter on low speed for 30 seconds, scraping the bowl as needed.

Pour the batter into the prepared pans, dividing evenly. Shake pans gently to settle batter. Place pans in a triangular pattern in hot oven on the middle rack, making sure they don't touch. Bake for 20 minutes, then quickly change pan positions for even baking, switching from back to front and vice-versa.

Bake for 5 to 7 minutes longer, until cake layers are brown and puffy and a knife inserted in the center comes out clean, or until the cake pulls away from the sides of the pan. Remove from oven, place on a wire rack and cool in the pans for 10 minutes.

Carefully loosen the cakes from the pans, turn them out onto the wire rack, and cool completely, top side up.

Pineapple Icing

1 can (20 ounces) unsweetened crushed
   pineapple
½ cup granulated sugar
1½ cups milk
1½ cups half and half or heavy cream
1¼ cups granulated sugar
½ teaspoon grated nutmeg or mace
1 teaspoon vanilla extract
3 large egg yolks
4 tablespoons unsalted butter, chilled and cut
   into pieces.

Fruit and Nut Filling

1 cup dried cherries, cranberries, apricots, plums,
   or peaches or a combination of fruits
¼ cup bourbon or dark rum, or more if desired
⅔ cup shelled pecans

In a medium saucepan, combine the crushed pineapple, juice from can, and ½ cup sugar. Bring to a boil, stirring. Reduce heat to medium low and cook uncovered, stirring occasionally, for 25 to 30 minutes or until liquid evaporates and pineapple is syrupy.

Meanwhile, combine milk, half and half or heavy cream, 1¼ cup sugar, nutmeg or mace, and vanilla extract in another large heavy saucepan and bring to a gentle boil, stirring. Reduce heat to medium and cook for about 15 to 20 minutes, or until the mixture is thick and syrupy, stirring occasionally.

Place egg yolks in a bowl and beat briskly with a whisk. Stir in a few tablespoons of the hot milk mixture and whisk again. Add another cup of hot milk to the yolks and whisk briskly.

Add egg yolk mixture back into the pan with the remaining milk and cook 5 minutes longer over medium heat, stirring constantly. Watch carefully and don't allow icing to boil; the eggs will scramble.

When the icing has thickened, immediately remove from heat and pour through a strainer into a large bowl. Beat in the butter and then the pineapple, mixing well.

Cool completely, stirring from time to time. If it's a little thin, chill for several hours until it is of spreading consistency, or set in an ice water bath.

To prepare the filling: Finely chop the dried fruit and combine with bourbon or rum in a small saucepan. Place pan on medium heat and cook for 5 to 7 minutes, stirring, or until the dried fruit is just tender.

Remove the pan from the heat. Coarsely chop the pecans, mix with the dried fruit, and set aside.

To assemble the cake: Set aside about ¼ to ⅓ cup of the fruit filling to use as a decorative topping. Place one cake layer top side down on a cake platter. Spread with about ¾ cup of pineapple icing. Scatter ½ the pecan and dried fruit mixture over it.

Put the second layer on top and spread with ¾ cup of icing and remaining fruit-nut mixture.

Put third layer on top, and spread the cake all over with the rest of the icing. With the reserved fruit-nut mixture, make a border around the edge of the top. Refrigerate for about 30 minutes to set icing.

Before serving remove from refrigerator and allow to warm to room temperature.

NEW YEAR'S DAY BUFFET

Sweet Goat Cheese Turnovers with Pistachios and Honey

Tom Douglas/Reprinted from *Tom's Big Dinners* (HarperCollins Publishers)

Serves 6

Frying these turnovers in olive oil makes them especially delicious—and very Greek.
Use pure olive oil, not extra virgin, because it has a higher smoke point.

8 ounces soft fresh goat cheese
1 tablespoon heavy cream
5 tablespoons sugar
2 teaspoons grated lemon zest
1 large egg yolk
1 tablespoon water
18 to 20 circles turnover pastry dough
   (recipe follows)
Pure olive oil, as needed for frying
½ cup chopped toasted pistachios
⅓ cup flavorful honey, as needed
½ cup fresh mint leaves

To make the goat cheese filling: in a bowl, beat the goat cheese with the cream, sugar, and lemon zest, using a rubber spatula or wooden spoon, until combined.

To make the egg wash: in a small bowl, beat the egg yolk and water together with a fork until just combined.

Lay the pastry circles out on a lightly floured work surface. Put a heaping teaspoon (about 2 level teaspoons) of filling in the center of a circle. Using a pastry brush, brush egg wash all around the edge, then fold over to form a half-moon turnover, pressing with a fork to seal. Continue to fill and shape all the turnovers in the same manner, and set aside on a parchment-lined or greased baking sheet.

Fill a heavy saucepan with oil to a depth of at least 1 inch. Heat the oil to between 325 and 350 degrees F, using a deep-fry thermometer. Fry the turnovers in batches as necessary, turning them to brown both sides. If oil is too hot, the turnovers may brown before the dough is cooked through. It should take at least 3 minutes to brown on both sides. If they are browning too fast, turn the heat down a little. As they finish, remove with a slotted spoon or skimmer and drain on paper towels.

To serve, arrange the turnovers on a large platter. Drizzle with honey and sprinkle with the chopped pistachios. Tear the mint leaves and scatter them over the top; serve immediately.

continued

Turnover Pastry Dough
Makes about 20 pastry circles

2½ cups all-purpose flour
2 tablespoons sugar
1 teaspoon kosher salt
1 cup (2 sticks) cold unsalted butter, cut into
    pieces
6 to 8 tablespoons ice water, or more as needed

Place flour, sugar, and salt in the bowl of a food processor. Pulse to mix. Add the cold butter all at once and pulse a few times until the crumbs form. Transfer the mixture to a bowl and start adding the ice water, one or two tablespoons at a time, mixing with a fork or rubber spatula. Add only as much water as is needed for the dough to hold together when a clump is gently pressed between your fingers. Dump the dough out onto a large piece of plastic wrap. Use the plastic wrap to gather the dough together and force it into a flattened round. Chill the plastic-wrapped dough about an hour or longer before rolling it out.

When you are ready to roll out the dough, unwrap it, place it on a lightly floured work surface, and cut it in half. With a lightly floured rolling pin, roll half the dough out into a rough circle about ⅛ inch thick. Use a 4-inch biscuit cutter to make 9 or 10 circles, setting them aside on a piece of parchment or wax paper. Repeat with the rest of the dough for a total of 18 to 20 circles.

Charcoal Grilled Lamb Skewers with Red Wine and Honey Glaze

Tom Douglas/Reprinted from *Tom's Big Dinners* (HarperCollins Publishers)

Serves 6

This richly flavored red wine and honey glaze also works beautifully with lamb t-bone chops or grilled steak. These lamb skewers marinate several hours or a day ahead, so plan accordingly.

2 pounds boneless leg of lamb, cut into 1-inch chunks
6 (10-inch) bamboo skewers, soaked in water for 30 minutes and drained
¹/₂ recipe Greek Marinade (see page 40)
1 tablespoon unsalted butter
2 tablespoons minced shallots
2 cups dry red wine, such as Cabernet Sauvignon
2 tablespoons honey
Kosher salt and freshly ground black pepper
¹/₂ recipe Parsley Salad (see page 41)

Thread the lamb chunks on the bamboo skewers and place them in a non-reactive pan. Pour the Greek Marinade over the lamb, turning the skewers to coat. Cover the pan with plastic wrap and marinate in the refrigerator 6 hours or overnight.

To make the red wine and honey glaze, melt the butter in a saucepan over medium-high heat and sauté the shallots a few minutes until lightly browned. Add the red wine, increase the heat to high, and boil until the wine is syrupy and reduced. You should have about ¹/₃ cup of reduced wine. Whisk in the honey, season to taste with salt and pepper, and cook the glaze another minute. Remove from heat and allow to cool. (You can make the glaze up to a day or two ahead and store it, covered, in the refrigerator. Allow the glaze to come to room temperature before using.)

When you are ready to cook the skewers, fire up the grill. Remove the lamb from the refrigerator and bring the meat to room temperature. Remove skewers from the marinade, shaking off excess. Season skewers on both sides with salt and pepper. Grill the lamb over direct heat, with the lid off, turning frequently with tongs. Brush with the glaze as you turn the skewers, using up all the glaze, until the lamb is done to your liking. The skewers will take about 7 to 8 minutes for medium rare, depending on how hot your fire is.

To serve, pile the skewers on a plate and top with the Parsley Salad.

Greek Marinade

Makes about 1¼ cups

1 tablespoon plus 1 teaspoon minced garlic
1 tablespoon plus 1 teaspoon dried Greek
    oregano, or other fragrant dried oregano
2 teaspoons freshly grated lemon zest
3 tablespoons Metaxa brandy
1 teaspoon kosher salt
1 teaspoon freshly ground black pepper
⅔ cup extra virgin olive oil

In a bowl, whisk together the garlic, oregano, lemon zest, brandy, salt, and pepper. Gradually whisk in the olive oil.

You can make the marinade a day or two ahead and store it, covered, in the refrigerator.

Parsley Salad

Makes about 3 cups

1 large bunch of parsley, leaves picked from the stems, washed and dried well (about 3 cups picked leaves)

½ lemon

1 tablespoon extra virgin olive oil

Kosher salt and freshly ground black pepper

Put the parsley leaves in a bowl. Squeeze the lemon over the parsley and toss. Drizzle the oil over the parsley and toss again. Season to taste with salt and freshly ground black pepper.

You can pick off and wash the parsley leaves a day ahead and store, covered with a damp kitchen towel, refrigerated. Toss the salad right before you serve it.

Grilled Shrimp and Garlic-Stuffed Black Olive Skewers

Tom Douglas/Reprinted from *Tom's Big Dinners* (HarperCollins Publishers)

Serves 6

Don't throw away the garlic flavored oil that is left after you cook the cloves—
it can be useful in many other recipes calling for garlic oil.

18 peeled garlic cloves
¼ cup olive oil, plus more for oiling the grill
18 large black olives, such as kalamatas,
    pitted and left whole
18 large prawns (16/20), about 1 pound, shelled
    and deveined, tails on
6 (10-inch) bamboo skewers, soaked in water for
    30 minutes and drained
½ recipe Greek Marinade (see page 38)
Kosher salt and freshly ground black pepper
½ lemon
½ recipe Parsley Salad (see page 38)

In a small saucepan, cover garlic cloves with ¼ cup olive oil and bring to a simmer over medium heat. As soon as the oil simmers, turn heat to very low and cook, stirring occasionally, until garlic is soft and very lightly browned, about 10 to 12 minutes. Drain the garlic cloves and set aside, reserving the garlicky oil for another use. Stuff each pitted olive with a garlic clove, cutting the olive open a little if necessary. Nestle a stuffed olive into the curve of each prawn.

Thread three olive-stuffed prawns onto each skewer. Be sure to pass the skewer first through the tail of the prawn, then through the garlic-stuffed olive, then through the head of the prawn so that everything is securely skewered.

Fire up the grill, or heat a grill pan.

Place the skewers in a non-reactive pan, cover with marinade, and marinate for 15 to 30 minutes. Remove them from the pan, shaking off excess marinade, and season on both sides with salt and pepper.

Brush the grill with oil. Grill the skewers over direct heat, with the lid off, turning them as needed, until cooked through, about 4 minutes. If you're not sure whether they're cooked through, take a skewer off the grill and cut through the thickest part of a prawn with a small knife—it should be opaque all the way through. Squeeze the lemon over the skewers right before you remove them from the grill.

To serve, pile the skewers on a platter and top with Parsley Salad.

LIGHT AND LEAN
FOR THE
NEW YEAR

Chilled Poached Gulf Shrimps with Zucchini and Dill Buttermilk Sauce

Judson Simpson, CCC

Serves 8

In this recipe, ribbons of zuchinni are delicately tossed with a refreshing combination of creamy yogurt and dill. Served in a martini glass, this appetizer makes a stunning addition to "cocktail hour."

2 ¾ pounds shrimp (21/25), peeled and deveined
4 cups court bouillon
4 medium green zucchini
1 cup buttermilk
½ cup light (1%) sour cream
½ cup light (1%) plain yogurt
1 tablespoon chopped dill
1 teaspoon Worcestershire sauce
Black pepper to taste
½ teaspoon salt
Lemon or lime wedges and fresh dill sprigs for
    garnish

Poach the shrimp in simmering court bouillon until cooked—just a few minutes. Remove from the cooking liquid, and allow both to cool. Place cool shrimps back in cooled liquid, and refrigerate until required. Shrimp can be cooked a day in advance.

To prepare the zucchini, slice them lengthwise into ribbons resembling fettuccini. Steam in a microwave or a stovetop steamer until tender crisp; cool.

In a medium or large bowl combine buttermilk, sour cream, yogurt, dill, chives, Worcestershire, black pepper, and salt until well mixed. Carefully stir in the zucchini.

To serve, place some sauce-coated zucchini on a plate and top with the chilled shrimp. Garnish with lemon or lime wedge and a sprig of fresh dill.

Court Bouillon
Makes 6 cups

6 cups water
½ cup dry white wine
2 stalks celery, coarsely chopped
    (include some leaves)
1 medium onion, coarsely chopped
1 lemon, cut in half (juice and rind)
3 bay leaves
1 teaspoon black peppercorns
1 tablespoon salt

Combine all ingredients in a medium sauce pot and simmer for 15 minutes. Before poaching shellfish, remove vegetables and lemon.

Clove-Spiked Citrus Chicken with Braised Spinach

Judson Simpson, CCC

Serves 10

Jud Simpson, the Executive Chef at the House of Commons in Ottawa, is an expert on healthy cooking and his creations continually debunk the myth of no-flavor low-fat cooking. Perfumed by the enticing aroma of whole cloves, this dish is as elegant as it is delicious.

10 boneless and skinless chicken breasts
   (about 3³⁄₄ pounds)
50 whole cloves
Black pepper
1 teaspoon extra virgin olive oil (for shallots)
1 large shallot, chopped
Juice of 2 large oranges
Juice of 2 red grapefruits
Juice of 2 limes
3 tablespoons honey
1 tablespoon cornstarch
¹⁄₂ teaspoon cinnamon
1 large navel orange, peeled, seeded, and diced
1 red grapefruit, peeled, seeded, and diced
1 tablespoon chives, chopped
1 teaspoon extra virgin olive oil (for red onion)
¹⁄₂ medium red onion, diced
20 ounces spinach, picked over
¹⁄₂ cup chicken stock
¹⁄₂ tablespoon thyme, chopped
1 teaspoon mustard seeds

Preheat oven to 375 degrees F.

Spike each chicken breast with 5 cloves and sear in a non-stick frying pan until lightly browned. Transfer to a baking sheet, bake at 375 degrees for 20 minutes.

To make the sauce, sauté the shallots in 1 teaspoon olive oil; add the orange juice, grapefruit juice, lime juice, and honey, and simmer for 5 minutes. Thicken with cornstarch and season with cinnamon. Add the diced orange and grapefruit and set aside, keeping it warm.

Sauté the red onion in 1 teaspoon olive oil on high heat until translucent. Add the spinach, chicken stock, thyme, and mustard seeds and cook until the spinach is just cooked.

To serve, place some of the braised spinach in the center of each plate; top with a chicken breast, and pour some sauce over the top.

Curried Beef Stew

Joyce White/Reprinted from *Soul Food: Recipes and Reflections from African American Kitchens* (HarperCollins Publishers)

Serves 4

Curry powder is the secret ingredient that makes this a very special beef stew. There's a wide range of curries available; try different ones before settling on a favorite.

4 pounds beef shanks
1 onion
2 to 3 cloves garlic
2 tablespoons vegetable oil
1 teaspoon salt
½ teaspoon freshly ground black pepper
2 tablespoons curry powder
1 cup beef broth
1 cup beer or water (more if needed)
1 medium all-purpose white potato

Cut the meat off the shanks and into 2-inch pieces, saving the bones. Slice the onion and mince the garlic.

Heat the oil in a large pot. Add the beef, a few pieces at a time so as not to crowd, and brown over medium-high heat for 4 to 5 minutes. As each batch is finished, remove it to a platter, sprinkle with salt and pepper, and set aside.

After the meat has all been browned, reduce the heat to low and add the onion and garlic to the pan. Sauté for 3 to 5 minutes.

Stir in the curry powder. Return both the beef and bones to the pot. Add the beef broth and the beer or water. Bring to a boil, cover, reduce the heat and cook over very low heat for 1 hour.

Peel and dice the potato and stir into the pot. Cover and simmer for 1 hour longer or until the meat and potatoes are tender and the beef broth is slightly thickened. Remove the bones and discard before serving.

Serve with rice.

Sautéed Garlic Greens

Joyce White/Reprinted from *Soul Food: Recipes and Reflections from African American Kitchens*
(HarperCollins Publishers)

Serves 6

*This recipe is very similar to the garlic-laden greens served in Brazil with the popular dish
called* feijoada, *a pot meal of pork, rice, and beans.*

3 pounds collard greens
1 large onion
2 or 3 cloves garlic
¼ to ⅓ cup vegetable oil
½ to 1 cup chicken broth
¾ teaspoon salt
½ teaspoon freshly ground black pepper

Pick over the greens and discard any with yellowing or wilted leaves. Remove thick stems. Stack a dozen or so leaves at a time and then roll tightly, jelly-roll fashion. Place on a cutting board and cut each roll crosswise into ½-inch strips. Continue rolling and cutting this way until all the greens are cut. Rinse the greens at least 4 or 5 times in a large basin of cold water, swishing to remove any sand or dirt. Drain well.

Chop the onion and mince the garlic.

Heat a scant 2 tablespoons or so of the oil in a large heavy pot. Place about a third of the greens at a time in the pot and sauté, stirring, for 5 or 6 minutes, or until the greens are wilted. Remove from the pot and set aside.

Add the remaining greens and 1 tablespoon of the oil and sauté in the same way. When all the greens are sautéed, add the remaining oil to the pot, stir in the onions and garlic, and sauté 4 or 5 minutes or until the onions are tender. Return all the greens to the pot.

Add the chicken broth, salt, and black pepper. Cover and cook over low heat for 30 minutes or until the greens are tender.

Orange Buttermilk Pie

Joyce White/Reprinted from Brown Sugar (HarperCollins Publishers)

Makes 1 pie (serves 6)

This unique dessert has a velvety texture that is livened up with a candied citrus topping.
The addition of buttermilk lends an unmistakable tang to the rich custard filling.
If you're pressed for time, use a high quality ready-made pie crust.

1 baked single pie crust
3 large eggs
1¼ cups granulated sugar
1 tablespoon all-purpose flour
1 tablespoon grated orange peel
1 teaspoon vanilla extract
½ to 1 teaspoon ground cinnamon
⅛ teaspoon salt
½ cup freshly squeezed orange juice
4 tablespoons unsalted butter, melted and cooled
1 cup buttermilk
¼ teaspoon cider vinegar or cream of tartar
2 to 3 tablespoons candied orange peel slivers

Prepare and fully bake a 9-inch pie crust according to recipe on next page.

Carefully separate the eggs into two separate small bowls, making sure that not one speck of yolk mixes in with the white. Transfer whites to a large spotlessly clean bowl (not plastic) for whipping, or to the bowl of a standing mixer. If an egg yolk drips into the white, discard it and break another egg, using a clean bowl.

Set aside the whites to warm to room temperature; return yolks to the refrigerator.

Preheat oven to 350 degrees F.

Transfer the egg yolks to a large bowl and beat briskly for a few seconds with a wire whisk. Add the sugar, flour, orange peel, vanilla, cinnamon, and salt, and whisk again. Whisk in the orange juice and butter and beat again until blended. Stir in the buttermilk and mix well. Set aside.

Sprinkle the vinegar or cream of tartar over the egg whites. Using the whisk attachment of a stand mixer, or a handheld electric mixer, beat the whites at medium high until they hold slight peaks. Stir a large spoonful of the egg whites into the filling and mix well. Fold in the remaining egg whites, and mix gently but thoroughly until blended. Pour into the prepared pie shell.

Bake on the lower rack for 35 to 40 minutes or until puffed and brown, firm, and a knife comes out almost clean when inserted.

Remove the pie from the oven, top with the candied orange peel. Cool on a wire rack and serve at room temperature.

Candied Citrus Peel (optional)
Makes 1 cup

3 large oranges or 4 large lemons
1 cup granulated sugar
1 cup water
1 tablespoon light corn syrup
½ teaspoon vanilla extract
¼ cup granulated sugar (for coating)

Rinse the fruit well. Using a small sharp knife or vegetable peeler, cut off the peel into ½-inch-wide strips, avoiding the bitter-tasting white pith. Cut the strips into matchstick slivers. Place in a medium saucepan, cover with cold water,

continued

bring to a boil, and blanch for 5 minutes. Drain, discard the water, and rinse with cold water. Return the peel to the pan, cover with cold water, and simmer for 20 to 25 minutes, or until just tender. Drain, rinse with cold water, and return to the pan. Add the sugar, water, corn syrup, and vanilla extract. Bring to a boil, stirring until the sugar dissolves. Cook the peel uncovered on low heat for 30 to 35 minutes, or until the syrup is thick and the peel is tender, translucent, and candied.

Pour the syrup and peel through a sieve and drain well. (Save the syrup; boil it down and use as a topping for ice cream or cake.)

Spread the well-drained peel on a sheet of wax or parchment paper and let dry in a sunny or warm spot for at least an hour. Sprinkle with the remaining sugar, and toss to coat. Transfer to a doubled sheet of paper towel, spread out and continue drying at room temperature for several hours.

Store the candied peel in an airtight jar or container. It will keep at room temperature for about 1 week; if keeping longer, refrigerate.

One-Crust Pie Shell
Makes pastry for a single 9- or 10-inch pie or quiche

**4 tablespoons unsalted butter, chilled, cut in
  1/2-inch pieces
3 tablespoons vegetable shortening, chilled
1 1/4 cups all purpose flour
1/4 teaspoon salt
3 to 5 tablespoons ice water, or as needed
1/2 teaspoon cider vinegar
1 lightly beaten egg white**

Put butter and shortening in a large, shallow mixing bowl. Sift the flour and salt into the bowl and mix well. Chill for 30 to 40 minutes.

Gather the chilled flour mixture in both hands and rub handfuls together briskly, letting it fall through your fingers. Alternate rubbing the dough with your fingertips until the mixture resembles coarse cornmeal. This should take no longer than 5 minutes.

Mix 3 tablespoons of ice water with the vinegar in a small cup. Sprinkle it over the dough 1 tablespoon at a time, lifting with a fork to dampen all over. Squeeze with your fingertips; if it doesn't hold together add more water, a tablespoon at a time.

When the dough just clings together but is not mushy and wet, quickly stir with a fork and gather into a disk or ball. Knead it with your hands a couple of times. Form the dough into a ball, dusting lightly with flour if it is sticky. Wrap the ball in plastic wrap or wax paper and chill for 30 minutes to an hour.

Preheat the oven to 400 degrees F.

On a lightly floured work surface, roll the dough into a 12-inch circle for a 9-inch pie pan, or into a 13-inch circle for a 10-inch straight-sided quiche or tart pan. Transfer to the pan, and fit carefully into the bottom and sides. Trim dough to 1/2 to 3/4 inch beyond the edge of the pan. Stand the overhang on the rim of the pan, and crimp or flute.

Cover the crust with a sheet of foil or parchment paper, and fill the pan with about 3 cups dried beans, or with pie weights. Bake for 18 to 20 minutes on the lower rack, or until crust is set and dry. Carefully remove the weights and the foil or paper. With a fork, gently prick any air bubbles in the crust. Bake 5 to 8 minutes longer, or until the pastry is golden brown and crisp. After 5 minutes watch the crust carefully, as it can burn quickly.

Ajiaco (Colombian Chicken and Potato Stew)

Bruce Weinstein and Mark Scarborough/Reprinted from *Ultimate Potato Book* (Chronicle Books)

Serves 6

Traditionally, two kinds of potatoes are used: baking, to thicken the stew, and yellow-fleshed, for texture. For lightness, we've left out the traditional cornmeal thickener. If you have a delicate palate, be careful with the hot sauce.

2 pounds yellow-fleshed potatoes, preferably fingerlings, such as Austrian Crescents or Russian Bananas, scrubbed

1½ pounds baking potatoes, preferably russets, scrubbed

2 tablespoons canola or other vegetable oil

1 large onion, finely chopped

1 (3- to 3½-pound) chicken, quartered

1 tablespoon minced fresh oregano

2 teaspoons fresh thyme

6 cups (1½ quarts) chicken stock

4 ears corn, kernels removed and reserved, cobs cut into thirds and reserved

½ cup finely packed chopped fresh cilantro

2 teaspoons salt

1 tablespoon lime juice

1 teaspoon hot sauce, or to taste

1 teaspoon freshly ground black pepper

Cut the yellow-fleshed potatoes into 1-inch cubes, or 1-inch rounds if using fingerlings. Place in a large bowl and cover with water. Peel the russets (but leave them whole), place in a second bowl, and cover with water.

Heat a large pot over medium heat. Swirl in the oil, add onion and cook until soft, about 2 minutes, stirring frequently.

Add chicken quarters and cook just until browned, about 2 minutes. Turn with tongs and sprinkle the oregano and thyme. Cook for 30 seconds, then pour in the stock. Bring to a boil, cover, reduce heat to medium-low, and simmer for 5 minutes

Drain the russets and finely grate them in the food processor. Add to stew and stir until it thickens, about a minute. Add the corncobs, cover, and reduce the heat to low. Simmer for 35 minutes, stirring often to keep the potato starch from scorching on the bottom of the pan.

Transfer the chicken pieces with tongs or a slotted spoon from the pot to a bowl and set aside. Remove corncobs and discard. Drain fingerlings and add to the stew. Cover and simmer for 10 minutes, stirring occasionally. Add the corn kernels and simmer, uncovered, for 5 more minutes, stirring often.

Meanwhile, remove the chicken skin and discard; take the meat off the bones and slice into bite-sized chunks. Return chunks to the pot, then stir in the cilantro, salt, lime juice, hot sauce, and pepper. Simmer for 2 minutes, until heated through, stirring constantly. Serve immediately.

It's hard to vary such a classic dish, so here are some simple toppings for it, once it's in the serving bowls: chopped cilantro; chopped red onion; corn relish; diced avocados; diced cucumbers; diced mangos; diced tomatoes; grated Cheddar or Monterey Jack cheese; plain yogurt; precooked cocktail shrimp; purchased salsa, particularly fruit-based such as peach or blueberry; sliced jalapeños; sliced pickled okra; sliced sweet pickles; sour cream.

CHINESE
NEW YEAR

Jiao-zi (Pork Dumplings)

Grace Young

Makes 30 dumplings. Serves 4 as part of a multi-course meal

Only in Northern China are jiao-zi *served in the hours between the old and the new year, affirming the wish for a prosperous year. Throughout China, the New Year's Eve dinner is the most important meal of the year, symbolizing thanksgiving and family unity.*

**2 cups all-purpose flour, plus additional for
    kneading**
8 ounces Napa cabbage
3 teaspoons salt
1 teaspoon sugar
8 ounces ground pork
1 tablespoon minced ginger
2 teaspoons soy sauce
1 teaspoon Shao Hsing rice wine or dry sherry
1 teaspoon oyster sauce
Jin Do's Tangy Ginger Sauce (see next page)

In a medium bowl, add ¾ cup cold water to 2 cups flour and stir until it begins to pull away from the sides of the bowl. Lightly dust a work surface with flour, and turn the dough out onto it. Knead briefly for 5 minutes with floured hands, adding more flour if necessary, until smooth. Cover with a damp cloth and allow to rest for 30 minutes.

Trim ¼ inch from stem end of the cabbage leaves. Stack a few leaves at a time and cut cross-wise into ¼-inch wide shreds, then finely chop. In a medium bowl combine cabbage, 1 teaspoon salt, and sugar. In another medium bowl combine the pork, ginger, soy sauce, rice wine or sherry, and oyster sauce. Add the cabbage, and stir until well combined. Cover loosely and refrigerate.

After the dough has rested, continue kneading on a lightly floured surface until dough is elastic and smooth, about 2 minutes. Roll into an even rope about 15 inches long. Cut into ½-inch pieces to form about 30 pieces. Roll each piece into a 1-inch ball. Pat the balls into plump 2-inch disks, lightly dusting with flour. Cover all unused dough with a slightly damp cloth. Using a floured rolling pin, roll back and forth over the edges of each disk, making the center slightly thicker, and the edges slightly thinner. The rounds will be about 3½ inches in diameter.

Place about 1 level tablespoon of pork filling in the middle of each round. Fold the round in half to form a half moon. Pinch one end of the half moon together. Using your thumb and index finger, make 4 or 5 pleats in the top piece of the dough only, as you pleat press together the edges. Then pinch together the other end of the half moon to seal. Stand each dumpling so the rounded edge is upright; place on a lightly floured tray.

In a 14-inch flat-bottomed wok, bring 3 quarts of water to a boil, covered, over high heat. When water boils, add 2 teaspoons salt and half the *jiao-zi,* and return to a boil, stirring gently with a wooden spoon. Add 1 cup cold water and return to a boil. Boil about 5 minutes or until pork is cooked through. Remove the dumplings with a slotted spoon, dividing among soup bowls. Repeat with remaining *jiao-zi.* Serve with Jin Do's Tangy Ginger Sauce.

After the *jiao-zi* have been eaten, ladle the hot *jiao-zi* liquid into the soup bowls.

Jin Do's Tangy Ginger Sauce
Makes about ³⁄₄ cup

3 tablespoons ginger, finely minced
¹⁄₃ cup Chinkiang or balsamic vinegar
¹⁄₄ cup soy sauce
¹⁄₄ cup sugar

In a small bowl combine ginger, vinegar, soy sauce, and sugar. Keep covered in the refrigerator for up to 5 days.

Linguine Nogada

Mark Scarborough and Bruce Weinstein/Reprinted from *Cooking for Two* (Morrow Cookbooks)

Serves 2

Nogada is a traditional Mexican sauce of walnuts and cream.
The cheese is quite salty; use additional salt sparingly. This vegetarian dish is best with a
fresh fruit salad dressed with a raspberry vinaigrette or poppy seed dressing.

1 tablespoon unsalted butter
1 small onion, finely chopped
¾ cup walnuts, finely chopped
½ teaspoon ground cinnamon
⅛ teaspoon grated nutmeg
2 tablespoons dry vermouth
½ cup heavy cream
6 ounces dried linguine, cooked and drained
according to package
2 tablespoons (about ½ ounce) grated queso
blanco or grated Monterey Jack
½ teaspoon salt (optional)

Melt the butter in a medium skillet set over medium heat, then stir in the onions and walnuts. Cook for about 2 minutes, or until the onions are golden and the walnuts are lightly browned, stirring frequently.

Stir in the cinnamon, nutmeg, and vermouth. Cook for just 20 seconds, or until the spices are fragrant; then stir in the cream. Bring the mixture back to a simmer and cook for about 2 minutes, or until the cream is thickened so it coats the back of a wooden spoon, stirring frequently.

Stir in the cooked linguine, the cheese, and salt if desired. Toss, then cook for just 20 seconds to heat through. Serve at once.

Pan-Seared Duck Breasts

Mark Scarborough and Bruce Weinstein/Reprinted from *Cooking for Two* (Morrow Cookbooks)

Serves 2

Elegant and flavorful, duck breasts are surprisingly easy to prepare. Here they are complemented with a delicate sauce of honey, vinegar, and fresh figs.

- **2 medium boneless duck breast fillets (about 10 ounces each)**
- **½ teaspoon freshly ground black pepper**
- **¼ teaspoon salt**
- **1 medium shallot, minced**
- **¼ teaspoon dried thyme, or ½ teaspoon fresh thyme**
- **1 small garlic clove, minced**
- **½ cup dry vermouth**
- **1 teaspoon Champagne vinegar or white wine vinegar**
- **2 teaspoons honey, preferably very aromatic honey, such as wildflower**
- **3 fresh figs, stemmed and quartered**

Position oven rack to middle; preheat oven to 350 degrees F.

With a sharp paring knife, score the skin and fat in the duck breasts to create a crosshatch pattern with ½-inch squares. Season with pepper and salt.

Heat a large, oven-safe skillet, preferably cast iron, over high heat until it is smoking. Add the breasts, skin side down, and immediately reduce heat to low. Cook for 6 minutes, or until golden. Shake the pan vigorously once or twice to keep the breasts from sticking. Turn over and cook an additional 3 minutes.

Place the skillet in the oven and roast for about 6 minutes, or until a meat thermometer inserted halfway into the thickest part of the breast registers 130 degrees F (for medium-rare, the preferred doneness); or for about 8 minutes, to 140 degrees F, for medium.

Transfer the breasts to a plate; tent with foil to keep warm. Pour off all but 1 tablespoon of the rendered duck fat. Place skillet over medium-low heat. Add shallot and thyme; cook for 2 minutes, until the shallot is softened and the mixture is very fragrant, stirring constantly. Stir in the garlic, cook for just 10 seconds, then pour in the vermouth and vinegar. Raise the heat to high and bring to a boil, scraping up any browned bits on the bottom of the pan. Boil for 2 minutes, stirring constantly, until reduced by half.

Swirl in the honey and cook for about 10 seconds, just until the honey melts, stirring constantly. Add the figs and cook for 10 more seconds, just until heated through. Remove from the heat.

To serve, slice the duck breasts into ½-inch thick slices. Arrange them on two plates, and divide the sauce between the two helpings. Serve immediately.

Note: fresh figs are delicate and sweet, but often hard to find. You can substitute 3 dried black Mission figs, soaked in hot water for 15 minutes until soft and plump, then drained, stemmed, and quartered.

Raspberry Almond Cheesecake

Mark Scarborough and Bruce Weinstein/Reprinted from *Cooking for Two* (Morrow Cookbooks)

Makes 2 individual cheesecakes

It may seem unusual that this recipe yields only two portions; it comes from the Cooking for Two *cookbook tailored for people who want just that. These light cheesecakes baked over flavorful almond crusts are so delicious, you just may want to double or triple the recipe.*

Unsalted butter for greasing the pans
¼ cup ground toasted almonds
8 ounces packaged cream cheese (regular or low-fat, but not nonfat), at room temperature
¼ cup sugar
1 medium egg or 5 quail eggs, at room temperature
1 tablespoon sour cream (regular, low-fat, or nonfat)
1 teaspoon all-purpose flour
½ teaspoon almond extract
¼ teaspoon vanilla extract
2 teaspoons raspberry jam
⅛ teaspoon hot water

Move oven rack to center, and preheat oven to 350 degrees F.

Generously butter the bottoms and inside walls of two 1½- to 2-cup ramekins, or two 4½-inch springform pans, or two 4-inch paper pastry shells. Spoon 2 tablespoons toasted ground almonds into each pan, and press into the butter on the bottom and sides to form a crust. Set aside.

Beat the cream cheese and sugar in a medium bowl with an electric hand mixer at medium speed for about 2 minutes, or until light and fluffy. Beat in the egg or quail eggs for 15 seconds, or until smooth; then beat in the sour cream, flour, almond extract, and vanilla for about 1 minute, until uniform. Gently spoon this mixture into the two almond crusts, dividing evenly.

Whisk the raspberry jam and hot water just until the jam melts. Dot this on top of the batter in each pan. Run a knife through the dots to create swirl patterns in the batter.

Bake for 30 minutes, or just until set. Turn off oven, prop the door open, and let cheesecakes sit inside for 30 minutes. Cool completely on a wire rack before unmolding. If you need to run a knife along the inside edges to loosen, take care not to separate the cheesecake from the almond crust. Cover tightly and refrigerate for at least 2 hours, or preferably overnight.

Chocolate Almond Cheesecake

Omit the raspberry jam and water. Instead, melt ½ ounce semisweet chocolate and 1 teaspoon heavy cream in a microwave on high for 1 minute, then continue stirring until the chocolate is melted. Dot this mixture over the cream cheese batter; drag a knife through the dots to create a chocolate swirl pattern.

VALENTINE'S DAY DESSERTS

Double Chocolate Sweetheart Cake

Rose Levy Berenbaum/Reprinted from *Rose's Celebrations* (William Morrow)

Serves 8

This cocoa layer cake, infused with a dark chocolate and cream glaze, is fudgy moist and soft within, and fabulously simple to make.

¼ cup plus 3 tablespoons unsweetened
   Dutch-process cocoa
⅔ cup boiling water
4 large egg yolks
¾ teaspoon vanilla extract
1½ cups plus 1 tablespoon sifted cake flour
   (sifted into the cup and leveled off)
1 cup superfine sugar
2½ teaspoons baking powder
½ teaspoon salt
9 tablespoons unsalted butter, softened

Chocolate Glaze
1 (3-ounce) bar bittersweet chocolate,
   preferably Lindt Excellence
¾ cup heavy cream
2 pints fresh raspberries
¼ cup red currant jelly

Whipped Cream
1 cup heavy cream
1 tablespoon sugar
½ teaspoon pure vanilla extract

Preheat oven to 350 degrees F.

Prepare a 9 by 2-inch heart shaped pan (8-cup capacity): Grease, line the bottom with parchment or wax paper, and spray with Baker's Joy (a spray available in stores that contains both flour and shortening).

In a medium bowl whisk together the cocoa and boiling water until smooth. Cover and cool to room temperature.

In another bowl lightly combine the yolks, ¼ of the cocoa mixture, and the vanilla.

Using your stand mixer, in a large mixing bowl combine the remaining dry ingredients and mix on low speed for 30 seconds to blend. Add the butter and remaining cocoa mixture. Mix on low speed until the dry ingredients are moistened. Increase to medium speed (high speed if using a hand mixer) and beat for 1½ minutes. Scrape down the sides. Gradually add the egg mixture in 3 batches, beating for 20 seconds after each addition. Scrape down the sides.

Scrape the batter into the prepared pan and smooth the surface with a spatula. The pan will be about half full. Bake 30 to 40 minutes or until a tester inserted near the center comes out clean and the cake springs back when pressed lightly in the center. The cake should start to shrink from the sides only after removal from the oven.

To make the glaze, break the chocolate bar into pieces and process in a food processor until very fine. Scald the cream and, with the processor running, pour the cream through the feed tube in a steady stream. Process a few seconds until smooth. Transfer the glaze to a small bowl and keep it warm. (Alternatively, grate the chocolate, place in a small bowl, and stir in the scalded cream until the mixture is uniform in color.)

When the cake is baked, place it, still in the pan, on a rack, and with a wooden skewer poke holes all over the top. With a brush, dabble half of the chocolate glaze onto the cake (this will take about 10 minutes). Cover a cardboard round or plate with plastic wrap or wax paper, and invert the cake onto it. Peel off parchment paper, poke holes as with the top, and dabble the glaze all over, and brush a little on the sides. Cool completely, for 1 hour or more, until the chocolate is firm to the touch. Invert the cake onto a plastic-wrap-covered 10-inch cardboard round or perfectly flat plate. Peel off plastic wrap, then re-invert onto a serving plate.

Place the raspberries closely together to cover the surface of the cake, starting at the outside border and working in toward the center. In a small heavy saucepan, melt the currant jelly over low heat. Use a small brush to paint the glaze over the raspberries.

If not using the raspberry topping, use a pastry brush to stipple the chocolate glaze as it is almost set, for an attractive textured appearance.

For additional garnish, whip the heavy cream with 1 tablespoon of sugar and $\frac{1}{2}$ teaspoon vanilla extract. Use a number 5 large star tube and pastry bag to pipe a shell border around the base of the cake.

Creole Shrimp and Andouille Stew with Rice

Susan Spicer

Serves 6 to 8

Making a "roux," an equal mix of flour to fat, is the secret to getting the lovely golden color and silky-smooth consistency for this common Creole dish. Be patient while cooking it, and your result will make any Creole cook proud.

4 tablespoons butter or cooking oil (or a combination)
4 tablespoons flour
1 cup chopped onion
½ cup chopped celery
½ cup green or red bell pepper, or mixed
1 tablespoon minced garlic
1¼ pound raw shrimp (21/25 count), peeled and deveined, cut in pieces, plus ¼ pound not cut
1 tablespoon chopped fresh thyme (chop leaves and reserve stems for bouquet garni)
1 pound Andouille sausage, split lengthwise and cut into pieces
1 quart broth of any kind (shrimp, chicken, vegetable)
1 tablespoon tomato paste
1 can chopped tomatoes
Bouquet garni made from bay leaf and stems of thyme and parsley
Salt and pepper to taste
Worcestershire sauce or hot sauce to taste

In a heavy-bottomed 4-quart pot over medium-high heat, melt butter and/or oil, then whisk in flour. Cook, stirring continuously, until roux turns the color of peanut butter, then carefully stir in the onion, celery, and bell pepper.

Reduce heat to medium. Add garlic, then chopped shrimp, then stir and cook until shrimp are pink. Add thyme and sausage, then whisk in broth, about ½ cup at a time. When all the broth is added, bring to a boil, whisking; then reduce heat to medium-low.

Whisk in tomato paste and chopped tomatoes, add bouquet garni, and cook, stirring from time to time, for 15 minutes, until stew is thickened and the flavor starts to develop. Season to taste with salt, pepper, and Worcestershire or hot sauce.

While stew is cooking, sauté the whole shrimp (peeled and deveined, but not chopped) in a little oil or butter, and add to stew just before serving.

Serve with hot rice mixed with chopped green onions.

Note: To make a bouquet garni, place the ingredients on a piece of cheesecloth approximately 4 inches square. Bring the 4 corners together above the herbs and with your other hand encircle just beneath, to make the neck of a small bag. Tie with string, making sure all edges of cheesecloth are captured, with no gaps below string. Remove from stew before serving and discard.

Oyster–Artichoke Gratin

Susan Spicer

Serves 4 to 6

No visit to New Orleans is complete without a sampling of some of the finest Louisiana oysters. If you can't make it to New Orleans, you can still find good oysters in many parts of the country.

2 fresh artichokes, trimmed and boiled, or 1 can artichokes, rinsed and chopped

1 pint oysters (approximately 24), shucked, with juices

1 tablespoon butter

Salt and pepper

1 cup breadcrumbs

2 tablespoons chopped Italian parsley

¼ cup (2 ounces) good quality olive oil

2 tablespoons melted butter

1 tablespoon grated lemon zest, and juice of one lemon

1 tablespoon chopped garlic

2 tablespoons chopped mixed fresh herbs, such as rosemary, thyme, and sage

¼ cup grana padano or Reggiano cheese

Preheat oven to 400 degrees F.

If using fresh artichokes, remove the choke and inedible leaves from the cooked vegetable, then slice or cut in wedges.

Pour oysters and their liquor into a bowl and remove any bits of shell.

Butter the bottom of an 8- or 9-inch pie pan or gratin dish and arrange oysters and artichokes in pan. Squeeze a lemon over the oysters and artichokes, removing any seeds. Season lightly with salt and freshly ground pepper.

Mix the breadcrumbs with all remaining ingredients and distribute evenly over the top, patting a little.

Place pan in the hot oven (or under a broiler) and bake for about 6 to 8 minutes or until crumbs are brown and bubbling. Remove from oven and serve immediately.

Bayona Spiced Pecans

Susan Spicer

Makes 1 cup

Susan Spicer, chef/owner of Bayona Restaurant in New Orleans, serves up these snacks to the city's keen residents and visitors. Smack in the heart of the French Quarter, this Louisiana mainstay features a bevy of imaginative Creole dishes.

1 cup whole pecans
2 tablespoons butter
1 tablespoon Worcestershire sauce
1 teaspoon salt
3 tablespoons sugar
¼ teaspoon cayenne pepper

Preheat oven to 350 degrees F.

Melt butter and toss with pecans and all other ingredients.

Spread coated pecans on a small baking sheet and roast in 350 degree oven until they are lightly toasted, approximately 5 minutes.

Store in an airtight container

Espresso Pots de Creme

Susan Spicer

Serves 12

Your guests will be charmed by this creamy custard dessert. The subtle coffee flavor and luscious rich texture is the perfect ending to a night of indulgence. Be sure to regulate the temperature of your oven carefully, to prevent the custards from drying out.

2 cups heavy cream
2 cups half and half
½ vanilla bean, split
5 ounces sugar
2 tablespoons instant espresso
6 egg yolks
1 teaspoon vanilla extract

Preheat oven to 275 degrees F.

Combine heavy cream, half and half, vanilla bean, and sugar in a large heavy saucepan. Cook over low heat until mixture reaches 180 degrees F. Use a candy thermometer to gauge temperature. Stir in the instant espresso until it is dissolved. Do not overheat.

In a large bowl, beat egg yolks lightly. Gradually add the hot cream, stirring gently and continuously to distribute heat so as to avoid scrambling the eggs. Keep stirring. Stir in the vanilla extract and adjust flavoring. Strain the mixture, then ladle into demitasse cups or ramekins.

To make a water bath, place a large, flat-bottomed baking pan on the oven rack. Place the filled ramekins in the pan, not touching each other, and then fill the pan with water halfway up the sides of the ramekins. Cover and bake at 275 degrees F for about 30 minutes, or until set. Centers will not be firm. At 25 minutes check that custard is cooking evenly and that edges are not browning. If edges are browning, turn the temperature down to 250 degrees F for 10 minutes.

Cool and refrigerate.

Serve at room temperature with whipped cream and chocolate-covered espresso beans.

AFTERNOON TEA

Cocoa Shortbread Fingers

Carole Bloom/Reprinted from *Chocolate Lover's Cookbook for Dummies* (For Dummies)

Makes 60 fingers

For extra added chocolate flavor, drizzle some melted chocolate on top after the shortbread is cool.

2 cups (4 sticks) butter, softened
1 cup sugar
½ teaspoon salt
½ cup unsweetened Dutch-process cocoa
   powder
3½ cups flour

Using a stand mixer, beat the butter in a large mixing bowl until fluffy, about 2 minutes. Add the sugar and mix together until smooth.

Combine the salt, cocoa powder, and flour together. Stir to blend well. Add to the butter mixture in 4 stages, stopping to scrape down the sides of the bowl after each addition. After all the dry ingredients are added, continue to mix for another 2 to 3 minutes, until the dough is smooth and soft.

Lightly flour a 9 by 13-inch baking pan. Dust your fingertips with flour and press the dough evenly into the baking pan. Use a ruler to score the dough into 1 by 2-inch bars. Use a fork to pierce each bar on the diagonal 2 times. Cover the pan tightly with plastic wrap and chill for at least 2 hours.

Preheat the oven to 275 degrees F and line a cookie sheet with parchment paper.

Cut through the scored lines on the chilled dough and place the bars on the cookie sheet, leaving 2 inches between them.

Bake for 40 minutes, until set. Remove cookie sheet from oven and transfer cookies to racks to cool. Store in an airtight container at room temperature for up to a week; freeze for longer storage.

Chocolate-Chunk Scones

Carole Bloom/Reprinted from *Chocolate Lover's Cookbook for Dummies* (For Dummies)

Makes twelve 3-inch triangular scones, or sixteen 1½-inch round scones

The chocolate chunks are a nice surprise in these scones. Although they're delicious on their own, they are superb served warm with butter and jam.

2½ cups flour
1 tablespoon baking powder
1 tablespoon plus 1 teaspoon sugar
⅛ teaspoon salt
6 tablespoons (¾ stick) butter, chilled
¾ cup (3 ounces) bittersweet or semisweet
  chocolate, chopped into small chunks
2 eggs
¾ cup heavy whipping cream

Egg Wash
1 egg yolk
2 tablespoons cream
2 teaspoons sugar

Preheat oven to 400 degrees F. Line two baking sheets with parchment paper.

Food processor method: In the work bowl of a food processor fitted with a steel blade, combine the flour, baking powder, sugar, and salt. Pulse briefly to blend. Cut butter into small pieces and add. Pulse until butter is cut into tiny pieces, 30 seconds to 1 minute.

Add the chopped chocolate and blend briefly.

In a small bowl beat the eggs lightly. Add the cream and blend well. Pour the mixture through the feed tube with the machine running and process until the dough forms a ball, about 30 seconds.

Stand mixer method: soften the butter to room temperature, then beat in a mixing bowl until fluffy. Add the sugar and cream together well. Lightly beat together the eggs and cream and add. Stop occasionally and scrape down the sides of the bowl with a rubber spatula. Combine the flour, baking powder, and salt together. Add to the mixture in 3 stages, stopping to scrape down the sides of the bowl after each addition. Add the chopped chocolate and blend.

Turn the dough out onto a lightly floured surface. Roll the dough or pat it with your fingertips into a large rectangle with a thickness of about ¾ inch. Brush off any excess flour. To form triangles, use a 6-inch diameter round cutter to cut out large circles, then cut each circle into quarters. To make round scones, use a 2½-inch round cutter. Transfer the scones to the lined baking sheets, leaving at least 2 inches space between them. Gather the scraps together, re-roll and cut into scones.

For the egg wash, beat egg yolk lightly in a small bowl with cream. Brush top of each scone with egg wash, then sprinkle with sugar. Bake for 12 to 14 minutes, until light golden. Remove from oven and cool completely on a rack.

Store the scones tightly wrapped in aluminum foil at room temperature for up to 3 days. Freeze for longer storage.

Dark Chocolate Nut Clusters

Carole Bloom/Reprinted from *Chocolate Lover's Cookbook for Dummies* (For Dummies)

Makes 3 to 3½ dozen clusters

The combination of hazelnuts, almonds, and dried cranberries creates a candy with lots of crunchy texture that's not too sweet. You can vary these by using milk or white chocolate and any combination of nuts and dried fruit you choose.

12 ounces (¾ pound) bittersweet or semisweet chocolate, finely chopped
1 cup toasted hazelnuts, coarsely chopped
1 cup slivered almonds, toasted
1 cup dried cranberries

Melt ¾ of the chopped chocolate (9 ounces) in the top of a double boiler over hot water, or in a microwave oven on low power for 30-second intervals. Stir often with a rubber spatula. Remove the top of the double boiler and wipe the bottom and sides very dry. In three stages, stir in the remaining chopped chocolate, melting each batch before adding the next. When all the chopped chocolate has been added, check the temperature by placing a dab just below your lower lip. It should feel comfortable, slightly cooler than body temperature. If it's too hot, stir in more chopped chocolate to bring down the temperature. If it's too cool, place the pan over the hot water again for a couple of minutes and stir to warm the chocolate.

In a large mixing bowl, combine the nuts and dried cranberries. Toss to mix well. Add to the chocolate and stir to coat completely with chocolate.

Line a baking sheet with wax paper. Spoon out clusters about an inch in diameter. When all the mixture has been scooped out, chill the baking sheet to set the chocolate, about 15 minutes.

Serve in individual paper candy cups at room temperature. Store the clusters between layers of wax paper in a tightly sealed container in the refrigerator for up to a month. Freeze for longer storage.

Chocolate Chiffon Cake

Carole Bloom/Reprinted from *Chocolate Lover's Cookbook for Dummies* (For Dummies)

Serves 14 to 16

This cake's deep flavor comes from the cocoa powder. Dust lightly with confectioners' sugar, or serve it with ice cream or a sauce and fresh fruit.

½ cup unsweetened Dutch-process cocoa powder
¾ cup boiling water
2 teaspoons pure vanilla extract
1¾ cups cake flour
1 tablespoon baking powder
½ teaspoon salt
1⅔ cups sugar
½ cup vegetable oil
6 eggs at room temperature, separated
½ teaspoon cream of tartar
Confectioners' sugar, for garnish

Preheat the oven to 325 degrees F. You will need a 10 by 4-inch tube pan with a removable bottom.

In a small bowl, combine the cocoa powder and boiling water. Stir until smooth, about 3 minutes. Let cool, then add the vanilla extract and stir to blend.

In a large mixing bowl, sift together the cake flour, baking powder, and salt. Add 1½ cups of the sugar. Stir to blend well, then make a well in the center of the ingredients, and add the oil, egg yolks, and chocolate mixture. Stir together until well blended.

In a large mixing bowl, use a stand mixer to whip the egg whites with the cream of tartar until frothy. Slowly add remaining ⅓ cup sugar and whip until the egg whites hold firm but not dry peaks, about 5 minutes.

Fold egg whites into the chocolate mixture in 4 stages, blending well after each addition. Pour into the tube pan.

Bake 60 to 65 minutes, until a cake tester inserted near the center comes out clean and the cake springs back when touched on the top. Remove from the oven and invert it onto a funnel to hang until cool. Release cake from the pan, using a thin-bladed knife or spatula to carefully run around the sides, and to remove the bottom and center core of the pan. Invert cake onto a rack, and re-invert onto a plate or cardboard cake round.

Dust the cake with confectioners' sugar before serving. Store tightly wrapped in plastic at room temperature for up to 3 days, or freeze for up to 4 months.

CENTERPIECE BREADS

Spicy Herbed Bread Sticks

Rose Levy Berenbaum/Reprinted from *The Bread Bible* (W.W. Norton & Company)

Makes about 68 bread sticks

Skinny as twigs, crisp, spicy, and herby, these are the ideal cocktail snack as they are enticingly flavorful but aren't too filling.

2¼ cups bread flour
½ teaspoon instant yeast
1⅛ teaspoons salt
1 teaspoon black pepper
½ teaspoon white pepper
½ teaspoon garlic powder
½ cup grated Parmigiano or Reggiano cheese, loosely packed
2 tablespoons minced herbs, such as chives, rosemary, thyme, sage, and/or marjoram
½ teaspoon hot sauce
1 cup water at room temperature
Cornmeal for dusting
Fine sea salt

You will need 3 baking sheets lined with parchment and sprinkled with cornmeal. Mix the dough 6 to 12 hours ahead.

If using a stand mixer, combine the flour, yeast, salt, black pepper, white pepper, garlic powder, grated cheese, minced herbs, and hot sauce in bowl. Use dough hook on low speed (#2 Kitchen Aid), to gradually add the water, then continue mixing just until the dough pulls away from the bowl. Do not overmix.

If mixing by hand, combine the flour, yeast, salt, black pepper, white pepper, garlic powder, grated cheese, minced herbs, and hot sauce in a large bowl. Mixing with a wooden spoon, gradually add the water, then continue mixing just until the dough cleans the sides of the bowl; do not overmix.

Transfer to a floured counter and knead it lightly, adding extra flour if the dough is at all sticky.

Place the dough in a lightly greased 1-quart bowl or dough-rising container. Push down and lightly spray the top. Mark the side of the container where height of doubled dough will be. Cover container with plastic wrap and refrigerate for 6 to 12 hours. After the first hour or two, gently deflate the dough; check again after a few hours and deflate again if the dough is rising more than double.

Put one oven rack at lowest level and another one level up. Preheat oven to 375 degrees F one hour before baking.

Cut the dough into 4 pieces, shape each one into a ball, then flatten each on a counter sprinkled with cornmeal. Work with two pieces of dough at a time, keeping the others covered and refrigerated. Pass one piece of dough through a pasta machine on the widest setting; the dough will be about ⅛ inch thick. Use cornmeal as necessary to keep dough from sticking.

Run the first piece of dough through the fettuccine (¼-inch size) cutter. Gently separate the strands, lay them on the cornmeal-dusted counter, and toss to coat them with the cornmeal. Lay the strands on prepared baking sheet, trimming to fit if necessary. Do not stretch or make them too thin. Leave a little space between the strands, which will expand during baking, to ensure crispness. Spray or brush with olive oil and dust each with a pinch or two of fine sea salt and more cornmeal.

Bake each batch for 12 to 16 minutes.

Mushroom Bread

Rose Levy Berenbaum/Reprinted from *The Bread Bible* (W.W. Norton & Company)

Makes one loaf, 8½ by 4 inches, with 5-inch "cap"

A bread steamer or a large coffee can works well to give this bread a mushroom shape. It makes a great display set on a bread board at the dinner table, and the "stem" cuts into beautiful rounds for serving.

You will need a glass bread steamer (4 by 6 ¼ inches) or 5-inch high coffee can, greased lightly with cooking spray or oil.

Dough Starter (Sponge)
1 cup bread flour
⅜ teaspoon instant yeast
1 teaspoon malt powder or barley malt, syrup, or sugar
1 cup water at room temperature

Flour Mixture
2 cups plus one tablespoon bread flour
2 tablespoons plus 2 teaspoons whole wheat flour
⅜ teaspoons instant yeast
1 cup duxelle mushrooms, firmly packed, at room temperature (see next page)
1 teaspoon salt

Early in the day or the night before, make the dough starter (sponge). In a large bowl (mixer bowl with whisk attachment if using a stand mixer) place the bread flour, yeast, malt or syrup or sugar, and water. Whisk (medium speed, #4 Kitchen Aid) until very smooth to incorporate air, about 2 minutes. The dough will be a thick batter. Scrape down the sides, and set aside covered with plastic wrap while making the flour mixture.

In a medium bowl, whisk together the bread flour (reserve ¼ cup if mixing by hand), whole wheat flour, and yeast. Gently scoop it onto the sponge to cover it completely. Cover tightly with plastic wrap and allow to ferment for 1 to 4 hours at room temperature. The sponge will bubble through the flour mixture in places.

With the dough hook, mix on low speed (#2 Kitchen Aid) until the flour is moistened, forming a rough dough. Scrape down sides of bowl. Cover with plastic wrap and let rest for 20 minutes. Add the salt and duxelles and mix on low speed (#2 Kitchen Aid) until the duxelles are incorporated. Increase speed to medium (#4 Kitchen Aid) and knead for 7 minutes. The dough should be very elastic and cool to the touch, and should jump back when pressed with a fingertip, but be moist enough to cling slightly to your fingers. If it is still very sticky, knead in a little more flour. If it is not at all sticky, spray it with a little water and knead it in.

With an oiled spatula or dough scraper, scrape the dough into a lightly greased 2-quart dough-rising container or bowl. Push down the dough and lightly spray or oil the top. Cover with a lid or plastic wrap. Mark with tape where double the height will be. Let rise (ideally at 75 to 80 degrees F) until doubled, 1 to 1½ hours.

Using an oiled spatula or dough scraper, scrape the dough onto a floured counter and press down on it gently to form a rectangle. Give it 1 or 2 business letter folds, round the edges, and set it back in the container. Oil the surface again, cover, and let it rise until doubled, about 30 to 45 minutes.

continued

When the dough has doubled, turn it onto a counter dusted lightly with flour. Roll it into a cylinder and push it down into the prepared bread steamer or coffee can. (If using the coffee can, fill only ⅔ full and reserve the remaining ¾ cup of dough for rolls.) Use your fingers to make sure it is pressed all the way down to the bottom. Cover it with a large container or oiled plastic wrap. Let it rise until doubled, about an hour, until when pressed gently the depression does not fill in. The highest center section should be 1½ inches above the top of the container and the dough should mushroom over the sides.

One hour before baking time, preheat the oven to 400 degrees F. Before preheating, place the oven rack at lowest level, and put a baking stone or sheet on the rack and a cast iron pan or sheet pan on the floor of the oven.

To bake, gently set the container on the hot baking stone or baking sheet. Toss ½ cup of ice cubes into the pan beneath. Immediately shut door and bake 55 to 65 minutes or until golden. Halfway through, for even baking, rotate the baking sheet or stone half a turn.

Remove the bread from the oven and unmold it onto a wire rack. For a shiny surface to the "mushroom cap," brush the top with 1 teaspoon of melted butter. Allow to cool completely, topside-up. Although this bread has a relatively low percentage of liquid it has a moist texture due to the duxelles. Well wrapped, it will stay fresh for up to 3 days at room temperature.

Duxelles

Makes about 1¼ cups, more than needed for the mushroom bread.

4 tablespoons butter
4 cups minced fresh white mushrooms, lightly packed (buy extra to allow for trimming)
1 medium clove garlic, lightly smashed
¾ teaspoon salt
⅛ teaspoon pepper

Clean and trim the mushrooms. Cut any large mushrooms in quarters first, then mince very fine, either by hand or with a food processor.

In a large skillet over medium heat, melt butter. Add mushrooms, garlic, and salt, and simmer covered on low heat for 5 minutes. Uncover skillet and continue to cook about 30 minutes, stirring occasionally, until the mushrooms turn dark brown and all the water has evaporated. Add more salt if desired. Stir in the pepper. Remove the garlic and discard it. Let cool to room temperature before adding to the dough.

ENTERTAINING
FOR
SPRING

Artichokes with Roasted Red Pepper and Olive Dip

Leslie Revsin/Reprinted from *Come For Dinner* (John Wiley and Sons)

Serves 6

The prize of the artichoke is the thick, fleshy saucer of a bottom. This dip is also excellent drizzled over grilled shrimp, salmon, or chicken, and as a sauce for roast pork.

3 thin slices of lemon
1 bay leaf
6 large globe artichokes
Salt and freshly ground pepper
1 cup coarsely chopped roasted red bell peppers
3 tablespoons coarsely chopped Piquillo peppers (see note)
2 generous tablespoons Dijon mustard, preferably French
½ cup plus 1 tablespoon extra virgin olive oil
Freshly squeezed lemon juice or wine vinegar, if needed
2 tablespoons coarsely chopped pitted ripe Mediterranean olives, such as Alfonso or kalamata
Hot sauce, if needed

Set a pot of water large enough to hold all the artichokes over high heat with the lemon slices and bay leaf. Meanwhile cut off 1 inch from the top of each artichoke with a serrated knife, cut the stems flush with the base, and discard trimmings. Cut off the thorny end of each leaf with scissors and set artichokes aside.

When the water boils, salt it generously and add artichokes. Cover and cook at a low boil for 20 to 25 minutes, depending on size. They are done when a leaf pulls out with very slight resistance.

Put the roasted red peppers, Piquillo peppers if using them, mustard, and olive oil in a blender or food processor. Puree until thick and somewhat smooth, about 2 minutes, scraping down the sides once or twice. (If using freshly roasted peppers, add a few drops of lemon juice or vinegar.) Season with salt and pepper, transfer to a bowl, and stir in the olives. If not using Piquillos, add a few drops of hot sauce, then set aside.

When artichokes are done, drain them upside down in a colander. As soon as they are cool enough to handle, gently squeeze their sides to remove excess water. Serve on plates, hot, warm, or at room temperature, with a spoonful of dip next to each or in individual tiny bowls. Place several empty bowls on the table for the discarded leaves.

Note: Spanish Piquillo peppers are gorgeous cardinal red with a charming triangular shape and remarkable depth of flavor—sweet with a touch of heat. In Spain they are roasted over a wood fire and stored in their own juices. If you don't have Piquillo peppers, increase the roasted red bell peppers to 1 cup plus 3 tablespoons. Jarred roasted peppers vary greatly in quality. They should be very red, appear firm, and not have citric acid as an ingredient.

Prepare the dip up to 4 days ahead; the artichokes up to 1 day. Store in refrigerator and remove an hour before serving.

Middle Eastern Beef
with Green Beans and Potatoes

Faye Levy/Reprinted from *Feast from the Mideast* (HarperCollins)

Makes 4 to 6 servings

If you're cooking with kosher beef, taste before adding any salt, as the meat has already been salted. And green beans are brightest if you cook them separately, but many cooks put them in with the potatoes to braise slowly and absorb the flavors of the sauce.

2 tablespoons vegetable oil or olive oil
2 large onions, halved and sliced thin
4 large garlic cloves, chopped
1 tablespoon ground coriander
1½ teaspoons ground cumin
½ teaspoon turmeric
½ teaspoon dried red chili flakes, or to taste
2 pounds beef chuck (shoulder), trimmed of
  excess fat, cut in 1-inch cubes
Salt and freshly ground pepper to taste
1 green bell pepper, cut in strips
4 ripe or canned tomatoes, diced
2 tablespoons tomato paste
1½ cups water
1 pound small or medium boiling potatoes
1 pound green beans, ends removed, halved
4 tablespoons chopped Italian parsley (optional)

Heat oil in a large stew pan, add onions and sauté over medium heat about 10 minutes or until brown. Add garlic, coriander, cumin, turmeric, and chili flakes and stir over low heat for 1 minute. Add beef, salt, pepper, and green pepper and cook over medium heat for 5 minutes, stirring often. Stir in tomatoes, tomato paste, and water and bring to a boil. Cover and cook over low heat for 1½ hours.

Peel potatoes if you like, and cut in 1-inch chunks. Add to stew. If stew appears dry, add ½ cup water. Cover and cook for 35 minutes, or until potatoes are nearly tender.

Cook green beans in a saucepan of boiling salted water for 5 minutes or until crisp-tender. Rinse with cold water. Add beans and 3 tablespoons parsley to stew and cook for 5 minutes or until potatoes and beans are tender. Taste and adjust seasoning. Serve sprinkled with the remaining parsley.

My Mother's Mushroom and Matzo Kugel

Faye Levy/Reprinted from *Feast from the Mideast* (HarperCollins)

Makes about 6 servings

This is a delightful side dish made with matzo, unleavened bread eaten during the Jewish holiday of Passover. It's available in most grocery stores and provides an interesting texture and taste to the casserole.

8 matzos
1½ cups hot chicken stock
5 tablespoons vegetable oil
2 large onions, chopped
1 celery stalk, cut in thin slices
8 ounces mushrooms, sliced
Salt and freshly ground pepper to taste
1 teaspoon paprika, plus a pinch for sprinkling
2 medium yellow squash, coarsely grated
Pinch of paprika or cayenne pepper
2 large eggs, beaten

Preheat oven to 350 degrees F.

Crumble matzos into a large bowl and pour hot chicken stock over them.

Heat 3 tablespoons oil in a large skillet. Add onions and celery and sauté over medium heat, stirring often, about 10 minutes or until golden. Add 1 tablespoon oil, then mushrooms, salt, pepper, and paprika, and sauté 3 minutes or until tender. Remove from heat and stir in squash. Add mushroom mixture to matzo mixture and let cool. Add hot pepper or paprika. Taste for seasoning. Stir in eggs.

Lightly oil a 2-quart casserole. Spoon kugel mixture into casserole, sprinkle with remaining oil, then with paprika. Bake for 45 minutes or until firm.

Queen of Sheba Chocolate Almond Cake

Faye Levy/Reprinted from *Feast from the Mideast* (HarperCollins)

Makes 8 servings

Like many Passover cakes, this is made with potato starch instead of flour. For meatless dinners, you can prepare it with butter instead of margarine. The cake is luscious enough to be served on its own but the chocolate truffle frosting adds extra richness.

1 cup blanched almonds
½ cup sugar
5 ounces semisweet chocolate, chopped
½ cup (4 ounces) unsalted margarine,
　cut in pieces
2 tablespoons water
4 large eggs, separated, at room temperature
2 tablespoons potato starch

Chocolate Truffle Frosting and Garnish (optional)
⅓ cup almond milk
4 ounces bittersweet or semisweet chocolate,
　finely chopped
¼ cup unsalted margarine
2 to 3 tablespoons chopped toasted pistachios
　or 8 to 10 toasted blanched almonds

Preheat oven to 325 degrees F. Lightly grease an 8 by 2 ½-inch springform pan with margarine, line base with parchment paper or foil, and grease paper or foil.

Grind almonds with 2 tablespoons sugar in a food processor until as fine as possible. Transfer to a bowl.

Combine chocolate, margarine, and water in a large bowl set above hot water over low heat. Stir until smooth. Remove from heat, cool slightly.

Whisk egg yolks to blend. Gradually add yolks to chocolate mixture, whisking vigorously. Stir in ¼ cup sugar, followed by almonds and potato starch. Mix well.

Whip egg whites in a large bowl until soft peaks form. Gradually beat in remaining 2 table-spoons sugar. Whip at high speed until whites are stiff and shiny but not dry. Gently fold whites into chocolate mixture in 3 batches, folding just until blended.

Transfer batter to pan and spread evenly. Bake about 1 hour or until a cake tester inserted in center of cake comes out clean.

Cool in pan on a rack for 10 minutes. Run a knife or metal spatula carefully around edges of cake. Turn cake onto rack, gently release spring, and remove pan. Remove paper and cool cake completely. Invert onto another rack, then onto a platter, so smoothest side faces up.

To make frosting, bring almond milk to a simmer in a small saucepan. Remove from heat and immediately add chopped chocolate. Stir quickly with a whisk until mixture is smooth; set it above a pan of hot water if chocolate doesn't melt completely. Let cool but do not let it harden. Beat mixture in a mixer at high speed for about 3 minutes or until color lightens.

Cream margarine in a large bowl until very soft and smooth. Gradually beat in chocolate mixture until frosting is smooth.

Spread frosting all over cake and smooth. Garnish center with pistachios or edge with almonds. Refrigerate for 2 hours before serving; serve at room temperature.

EASTER
CHOCOLATES

For the dark chocolate ganache layer, heat the cream to a boil in a medium saucepan. Remove from heat and stir in the chocolate until completely melted and smooth. Stir in the vanilla and blend well. Stir the mixture for a few minutes to cool.

Meanwhile, heat the cream and white chocolate together in a small saucepan for the white chocolate ganache, just until the chocolate is melted. Remove from heat and stir until smooth.

Pour the dark chocolate mixture into the tart shell. Working quickly, drizzle the white chocolate mixture over the dark chocolate mixture. Use a toothpick or the point of a sharp knife to pull through the white chocolate layer to marbleize. Chill until filling is firm, about 2 hours. Store tightly covered in the refrigerator for up to 2 days. Let it stand at room temperature for 30 minutes before serving.

White Chocolate–Apricot Truffles

Carole Bloom/Reprinted from *Chocolate Lover's Cookbook for Dummies* (For Dummies)

Makes 4 dozen truffles

Plump dried apricots are the perfect counterpart for white chocolate in these delicious truffles.

2 tablespoons water
2 tablespoons apricot brandy or orange liqueur
²/₃ cup dried apricots, finely chopped
12 ounces white chocolate, finely chopped
½ cup heavy whipping cream
4 tablespoons confectioners' sugar
1 pound white couverture chocolate, finely chopped, for tempering
48 slivers dried apricot

Bring water and orange liqueur to a boil over medium heat in a 1-quart saucepan. Stir in chopped apricots, cover, remove from heat, and let stand for 30 minutes. Strain the apricots and pat dry.

Melt the white chocolate over hot water in the top of a double boiler, or in a microwave oven on low power for 30-second intervals. Stir often with a rubber spatula to ensure even melting. In a separate small saucepan, scald cream over medium heat.

Remove the top pan of the double boiler and wipe bottom and sides very dry. Pour the scalded cream into the chocolate, and stir to blend until smooth. Stir in the apricots. Pour into a bowl, cover tightly with plastic wrap, and cool to room temperature. Refrigerate until the consistency of thick pudding, 2 to 3 hours.

Line a baking sheet with wax paper. Use a 14-inch pastry bag with a ½-inch plain round tip to pipe out 1-inch mounds of the truffle cream, or use a small ice cream scoop or melon baller. Cover with plastic wrap and chill in freezer about an hour, until firm enough to roll into balls.

When the truffle mounds are firm, dust your hands with confectioners' sugar and shape the mounds into balls. Cover and chill again while melting and tempering the chocolate.

Line another baking sheet with wax paper. Melt and temper the white chocolate (see page 116). Using a fork or dipping tool, dip each truffle center in the chocolate and gently shake off the excess as it is lifted out. Place the truffles on the baking sheet. After dipping 4 truffles, center a sliver of dried apricot on top of each. When all are dipped, chill for 15 minutes to set.

Serve truffles at room temperature. Store between layers of wax paper in an airtight container wrapped with aluminum foil in the refrigerator for up to 3 weeks or in the freezer for up to 2 months. If frozen, defrost in the refrigerator for a day before bringing to room temperature.

Solid Molded Chocolate

Carole Bloom/Reprinted from *Chocolate Lover's Cookbook for Dummies* (For Dummies)

Makes 24 pieces

Couverture chocolate is professional quality chocolate that contains extra cocoa butter, giving it more fluidity and making it ideal for dipping, molding, and decorating. It can be obtained in specialty candy-making shops, or check out the internet for mail-order sources.

1 pound couverture chocolate, finely chopped, for tempering

You will need 2 large paper pastry cones and two 12-cavity 1-inch chocolate molds.

Prepare the pastry cones. Put the molds on a flat work surface. Melt and temper the chocolate as described below.

Pour half of the chocolate into one of the cones. Fold down the top and snip off a ¼-inch opening at the pointed end. Pipe the chocolate into one of the molds, filling each cavity to the top. Repeat with the remaining paper cone and mold.

Tap the molds lightly on the countertop to remove any air bubbles, which will make holes in the chocolate when set. Put molds on a baking sheet. Chill on a flat surface in the freezer for 15 to 20 minutes to set.

Remove molds from the freezer and invert over a large piece of wax paper. To unmold, hold mold at opposite corners and twist gently. If chocolates don't drop out quickly, chill for another 10 minutes.

Add texture by stirring ¼ cup of any of these ingredients into the chocolate before molding: finely ground toasted nuts, toasted shredded coconut, finely chopped dried fruit, finely chopped crystallized ginger, or finely chopped candied orange peel.

Tempering

This method is also called the pot method of tempering. Although accuracy is important when tempering chocolate, this method doesn't rely on an exact temperature. This method is good if you're just getting started tempering chocolate.

For this method of tempering to be successful, you must start with tempered chocolate. Untempered chocolate pieces that are stirred into the melted chocolate will cause the batch to be untempered.

1. Chop 1 pound of chocolate very finely.

2. Place two-thirds of the chocolate in the top of a double boiler and melt over low heat, stirring frequently with a rubber spatula to ensure even melting.

Alternatively, melt chocolate in a microwave oven on low power for 15- to 30-second intervals. Stir between each interval.

3. Remove the chocolate from the double boiler (if using) and wipe the bottom and sides very dry. If using a microwave oven,

remove the bowl and stir the chocolate to make sure it's completely melted.

4. Stir in the remaining third of finely chopped chocolate in 3 batches. Make sure each batch is melted before adding the next. The chopped chocolate will absorb the heat of the melted chocolate and cool it.

5. When all the chopped chocolate has been added test the temperature of it by placing a dab of chocolate below your lower lip. It should feel comfortable—not too hot or too cool. If it's still too warm, add more chopped chocolate to cool it down. If it's too cool, place the bowl or pan of chocolate over warm water briefly to bring the temperature up.

GREEK EASTER DINNER

Greek Easter Bread

Christine Cushing/Reprinted from *Fearless in the Kitchen* (Viking Canada)

Makes one circular braided loaf

*Mahlepi is an unusual Greek spice with a distinctive fruity taste, made from the kernels of
fruit pits of a native Persian cherry tree. If you can't find it, allspice is a suitable substitute.
Masticha comes from the resinous substance of the Pistacia tree and is used to flavor baked goods.
If you can't find this in your area, you can substitute anise.*

1 cup bread flour
3 cups all-purpose flour
1 teaspoon salt
1 teaspoon ground anise
¾ teaspoon ground mahlepi (available at Greek
  food shops)
Grated zest of 1 lemon
½ teaspoon ground masticha (available at Greek
  food shops)
Grated zest of 2 oranges

¾ cup warm milk
3 tablespoons sugar
1½ packages active dry yeast

3 eggs
¾ cup sugar
¼ cup melted butter

½ to ¾ cup all purpose flour for kneading
1 beaten egg for brushing bread
1 hardboiled egg in red-tinted shell, for finish

In a large mixing bowl, use your stand mixer's
hook attachment to combine bread flour, all-
purpose flour, salt, anise, mahlepi, masticha, and
lemon and orange zests in.

In a small bowl, combine lukewarm milk
with 3 tablespoons sugar and whisk. Add yeast,
stir, and let stand 5 minutes or until frothy.

In a medium bowl whisk eggs, ¾ cup sugar,

and butter. Add yeast mixture to flour mixture
with mixer on low speed. Then add egg mixture
and mix on medium speed until dough is sticky.

Turn mixture out onto well-floured surface
and knead for about 10 minutes, using flour as
required. Dough should be smooth and elastic
but not sticky or dry.

Shape into a ball and let rest in a well-oiled
bowl covered with plastic for 2 hours or until
doubled in bulk.

Punch down and separate dough into 3
equal portions, shape into balls, and let rest, covered, for about 15 minutes.

Roll each ball into a strand about 28 inches
long. Braid the 3 lengths into one braid, and
tuck the ends under.

Transfer braid to baking sheet lined with
parchment paper, form into a circle, and fasten
ends together to form wreath. Nestle red-tinted
Easter egg at the seam.

Preheat oven to 350 degrees F.

Cover braided wreath and let rise in a warm
place for 40 to 50 minutes or until finger
imprint does not spring back. Brush with beaten
egg and bake on middle rack of preheated oven
for 35 minutes, or until it is brown and sounds
hollow when tapped on bottom.

Greek Easter Roast Leg of Lamb

Christine Cushing

Serves 8 to 10

This succulent recipe comes from television host and cookbook author Christine Cushing. She was born in Greece, where Easter is celebrated with joyful displays of cherished family recipes, over which roasted lamb presides. This dish is particularly well-suited for large gatherings.

1 leg of lamb (fresh or New Zealand Spring),
    about 3⅓ to 4½ pounds
¼ cup olive oil
4 cloves garlic, cut into slivers
Cracked black pepper, to taste
1 tablespoon coarse sea salt
4 to 5 sprigs fresh thyme, leaves only
1 tablespoon dried Greek oregano
Juice of ½ lemon
8 pearl onions, peeled and quartered
1 bay leaf

Orzo
4 cups chicken stock
2 1-pound packages orzo pasta

Preheat oven to 400 degrees F.

Prepare lamb by making small incisions about ½ inch deep evenly around surface of leg. Combine garlic in a small bowl with salt and pepper. Push garlic cloves into incisions. Rub leg generously with oil and lemon juice. Sprinkle with remaining salt and pepper, thyme leaves, and oregano. Transfer to a large roasting pan.

Roast for 20 minutes at 400 degrees, reduce heat to 350 degrees, and cook 45 minutes longer. Add pearl onions and roast for 20 to 35 more minutes, or until internal temperature is 140 degrees, for medium-rare. Remove lamb, wrap in foil, and set aside in a second pan. Add chicken stock and bay leaf to roasting pan and stir to remove crusty bits from bottom. Bring to a boil in oven and add orzo. Bake until most of liquid is absorbed , about 15 minutes. Remove lamb from foil and put back in roasting pan on top of orzo. Continue to roast until lamb reaches about 150 degrees internal temperature.

Serve immediately.

EARTH DAY

WEDDING CAKES

White Cake

Dede Wilson/Reprinted from *The Wedding Cake Book* (John Wiley & Sons)

Makes 2 6-inch layers

A very basic but versatile white cake, this will mix-and-match beautifully with any buttercream or filling.

2⅓ cups unsifted cake flour
1 tablespoon baking powder
⅓ teaspoon salt
4 large egg whites
1 cup whole milk
5⅓ ounces (slightly more than 1¼ sticks)
    unsalted butter, at room temperature
1⅓ cups sugar
2 teaspoons vanilla extract

Preheat oven to 350 degrees F. Prepare two 6 by 2-inch cake pans with cooking spray and parchment paper.

Sift together flour, baking powder, and salt, and set aside. Whisk together the egg whites and milk in a small bowl and set aside.

Use your mixer's flat paddle attachment to cream butter on medium-high speed. Add sugar gradually and beat until well blended. Scrape down the bowl once or twice; beat in the vanilla.

Add the dry ingredients and the egg white mixture alternately, scraping down the sides several times. Continue to beat on medium speed until just smooth.

Scrape batter into pans and bake about 40 to 50 minutes, or until a toothpick tests clean. Edges will be slightly brown and will begin to pull away from sides of pans. Cool, place on cardboards, and wrap with plastic wrap and foil until ready to frost.

For two 8 x 10-inch layers
3½ cups unsifted cake flour
1 tablespoon plus 1 teaspoon baking powder
½ teaspoon salt
6 large egg whites
1½ cup whole milk
8 ounces (2 sticks) unsalted butter, at room
    temperature
2 cups sugar
1 tablespoon vanilla extract

Prepare two 8 x 2-inch cake pans with cooking spray and parchment paper. Proceed as for 6-inch layers. Bake about 40 to 50 minutes.

For two 9 x 2-inch layers
4⅔ cups unsifted cake flour
2 tablespoons baking powder
⅔ teaspoon salt
8 large egg whites
2 cups whole milk
10⅔ ounces (slightly more than 2½ sticks)
    unsalted butter, at room temperature
2⅔ cups sugar
1 tablespoon plus 1 teaspoon vanilla extract

Prepare two 9 x 2-inch cake pans with cooking spray and parchment paper. Proceed as for 6-inch layers. Bake about 45 to 55 minutes.

continued

For two 10 x 2-inch layers
5 3/4 cups plus 1 tablespoon unsifted cake flour
2 tablespoons plus 2 teaspoons baking powder
3/4 teaspoon salt
10 large egg whites
2 1/2 cups whole milk
13 1/2 ounces unsalted butter, at room
   temperature
3 1/2 cups sugar
1 tablespoon plus 2 teaspoons vanilla extract

Prepare two 10 x 2-inch cake pans with cooking
spray and parchment paper. Proceed as for 6-
inch layers. Bake about 45 to 55 minutes.

For two 12 x 2-inch layers
Make the 9-inch cake recipe twice, once for each
12 x 2-inch cake. Bake about 50 to 60 minutes.

For two 14 x 2-inch layers
Make the 10-inch cake recipe twice, once for
each 14 x 2-inch cake. Bake about 55 to 65 minutes.

Mexican Salsa *(Salsa Mexicana)*

Rafael Palamino/Reprinted from *Nueva Salsa* (Chronicle Books)

Makes about 2½ cups

Chipotle—smoked jalapeño chiles—is fiery, but doesn't distract from other flavors. And you can always adjust the amount of chipotle according to your own taste.

2 roasted tomatoes (see page 135), coarsely chopped

1 roasted red onion (see page 135), coarsely chopped

2 ripe Hass avocados, peeled, pitted, and coarsely chopped

Kosher salt and freshly ground pepper to taste

2 teaspoons white balsamic vinegar

1 tablespoon chipotle puree (right) or rocoto paste

Juice of 1 lime

2 tablespoons coarsely chopped fresh cilantro

In a large bowl combine the tomatoes, onion, and avocados. Toss gently. Gently stir in the salt, pepper, vinegar, oil, chipotle puree or rocoto paste, and lime juice. Let sit for about 20 minutes, then stir in the cilantro and serve. Or, cover and refrigerate for up to 1 day. Return to room temperature and stir in the cilantro just before serving.

Chipotle Puree

Empty a can of *chipotles en adobo* into a blender or food processor and blend until smooth. Cover and store in the refrigerator for up to 6 months. One 13 ½-ounce can of *chipotles en adobo* makes about 10 ounces chipotle puree.

MOTHER'S DAY

Sweet Vidalia Onion and Gruyère Soufflé

Maria Helm Sinskey/Reprinted from *The Vineyard Kitchen* (HarperCollins)

Makes two 1-quart soufflés; serves 8 as an appetizer, 4 as a light supper

*Sweet Vidalias arrive in midspring. If you can't find Vidalias,
substitute another sweet spring onion or a sweet cured onion.*

Unsalted butter (at room temperature) and ⅔ cup
finely grated Parmesan cheese to line soufflé
molds
¾ pound Vidalia onions or other sweet onions,
spring or cured (see above)
9 tablespoons unsalted butter
2 teaspoons packed chopped fresh thyme or
1 teaspoon dried
Salt
Freshly ground black pepper
½ cup all-purpose flour
2½ cups whole milk
6 large eggs, separated
1½ cups grated Gruyère cheese
½ cup finely grated Parmesan cheese

Butter two 1-quart soufflé dishes. Cut a strip of parchment paper 5 inches wide and long enough to fit the inside wall of soufflé mold, with ends overlapping, and the top of paper extending 2 inches above the edge of mold. Butter both sides of parchment and press against the inside of mold. Place ⅓ cup of Parmesan into each mold and roll until thoroughly coated.

Trim spring onions and dice finely. If using cured onions, peel first. Heat 1 tablespoon of butter in a sauté pan over medium-high heat until lightly browned. Add diced onions and cook until lightly caramelized, 5 to 6 minutes. Add chopped thyme and season with salt and pepper. Cool and reserve at room temperature.

Melt 8 tablespoons of butter in a heavy-bottomed saucepan over medium heat. Add flour and stir constantly until well combined. Remove from heat and gradually add milk, stirring constantly. When adding milk, mix the batter until smooth before adding more. Add 1 teaspoon of salt and a few grinds of black pepper. Place pan back on heat and stir until mixture is smooth and pulls away from sides of pan.

Transfer this soufflé base into mixing bowl of a stand mixer. Mix on medium speed using the paddle attachment. Add yolks one at a time, increasing speed to high for 10 seconds. Return to medium speed to add the next yolk; repeat until all yolks are incorporated. After the last yolk, beat for 20 seconds on high. Scrape down sides of bowl. Return to medium speed. Stir in cheese and onion until well combined.

Turn batter out into a large mixing bowl and press plastic wrap against the surface. Store at room temperature for up to 4 hours. If you refrigerate the batter, bring it up to room temperature before incorporating the egg whites, or your soufflé will be flat.

Preheat the oven to 400 degrees F.

Using a stand mixer or hand mixer, beat egg whites to stiff peaks on high with ½ teaspoon of salt. Fold in thirds into prepared soufflé base and mix lightly until whites are incorporated. A few white streaks are acceptable. Spoon into molds, almost to top of dish. Bake until well puffed and golden, 35 to 40 minutes.

For smaller soufflés, line 10 small molds in the same manner as the large molds but without the collar. Bake for 20 to 30 minutes at 400 degrees F.

Herb-Marinated Rack of Lamb with Roasted Garlic Fingerling Potatoes

Maria Helm Sinskey/Reprinted from *The Vineyard Kitchen* (HarperCollins)

Serves 8

The herb marinade for the lamb really perfumes the meat when done a day or two ahead of time. Remove herbs and garlic before roasting the meet; they will burn and change the flavor.

4 lamb racks, 8 to 9 ribs each
½ cup plus 2 tablespoons extra virgin olive oil
8 large whole garlic cloves, unpeeled and crushed, plus 16 large whole unpeeled garlic cloves
12 (4-inch) fresh rosemary sprigs or 4 tablespoons dried rosemary
12 fresh thyme sprigs or 1 tablespoon dried thyme
Freshly ground black pepper
3 pounds fingerling potatoes
3 tablespoons coarse sea salt
Salt to taste

Marinate the lamb racks the day before roasting and serving.

Scrape rib bones clean of the meat and sinew with a small sharp knife. Cut racks in half. In a large bowl, combine ¼ cup olive oil and the 8 crushed garlic cloves. Hand-crush the rosemary and the sprigs and add. Add the lamb and coat well. Coarse-grind black pepper over all. Cover well and marinate overnight.

Preheat the oven to 400 degrees F.

Scrub potatoes under running water and drain well. If potatoes are large, cut in half lengthwise.

In a big bowl, toss the potatoes, the 16 whole garlic cloves, coarse sea salt, and ¼ cup olive oil together; season with freshly ground black pepper.

Spread the potatoes in one layer on a baking sheet or roasting pan and put in oven 15 minutes before lamb racks. The potatoes need to roast until they are tender and golden.

Remove lamb from marinade and scrape off as many herbs as possible. Heat a large oven-proof sauté pan over medium-high heat; add remaining 2 tablespoons of olive oil.

Season the lamb well with salt and sear fat side down until golden, about 7 minutes. Turn racks over so that fat side is up and roast in the oven for 20 to 30 minutes. When done, remove lamb from oven and let it rest on a platter or cutting board for 10 minutes, then cut each rack in half. The potatoes can continue to roast while the lamb is resting; if they are done, remove from oven and cover with foil to keep them warm.

Serve the lamb on a platter surrounded with the roasted potatoes.

Caramelized Rum-Scented Bananas with Bittersweet Chocolate Sauce

Maria Helm Sinskey/Reprinted from *The Vineyard Kitchen* (HarperCollins)

Serves 8

Serve the bananas with chocolate sauce and some toasted nuts and you will swear you are eating a banana split or a fancy version of Bananas Foster.

8 large ripe but firm bananas
6 tablespoons unsalted butter
³⁄₄ cup sugar
³⁄₄ cup dark rum
Bittersweet Chocolate Sauce
Toasted almonds (optional)

Preheat oven to 250 degrees F. Lightly butter a sheet pan and keep it handy to hold the cooked bananas.

Peel and slice bananas ¹⁄₂ inch thick on the diagonal. Heat 2 tablespoons butter over high heat in a heavy-bottomed pan until it bubbles and turns golden. Add a third of the bananas and cook until they are golden brown on the edges. Turn the bananas over and brown the other side. Sprinkle with ¹⁄₄ cup of sugar and cook until the sugar is caramelized and dark gold in color.

Remove pan from heat or turn off flame, and add ¹⁄₄ cup of rum. Keep the pan away from your face and other flammable objects. Place it back on the heat and shake the bananas. Be careful! The run could flame at any time. Do not lean over the pan. Simmer until the rum has reduced to a syrup, about 3 minutes. Pour the caramelized bananas onto the buttered sheet pan and place in the preheated oven to keep warm. Repeat with the remaining bananas.

Serve in bowls drizzled with chocolate sauce and topped with a sprinkle of toasted almonds. Another way to serve is to put a scoop of vanilla ice cream in the bowl first, top with warm bananas, then chocolate sauce and almonds.

Note: When working with caramelized sugar, keep a big bowl of ice water nearby. If any hot sugar splatters on your hands, plunge into ice water to lessen burning.

Bittersweet Chocolate Sauce
Makes 2 cups

8 ounces bittersweet chocolate (70 percent cocoa solids)
1 cup heavy cream
¹⁄₄ cup whole milk
1 ounce good rum (optional)
4 tablespoons unsalted butter, at room temperature

Finely chop the chocolate and place in a 2-quart bowl.

Bring the cream, milk, and rum to a boil in a heavy-bottomed saucepan. Turn off the heat and cool slightly.

Slowly pour the milk-cream mixture into the chopped chocolate, stirring rapidly. Stir until well combined.

Stir in the butter until it is completely incorporated. Store at room temperature for 1 day, otherwise refrigerate for up to a month. To serve, warm slightly until pourable.

MEMORIAL DAY
BARBECUE

Baby Back Barbecue Ribs

Pat Schweitzer and Betty Morton/Reprinted from *Pat and Betty's No-Fuss Cooking* (Hyperion)

Serves 5

Here is a quick and easy way to prepare one of America's favorite backyard treats, barbecued ribs. Packet cooking seals in the moisture and flavor, and clean-up couldn't be easier.

2 sheets (18 by 24 inches each) Reynolds Wrap® Heavy Duty Aluminum Foil

3 pounds baby back pork ribs

1 tablespoon packed brown sugar

1 tablespoon paprika

2 teaspoons garlic powder

1½ teaspoons pepper

½ cup water or 6 to 8 ice cubes

1½ cups barbecue sauce

Preheat grill to medium.

Center half of ribs in a single layer on each sheet of aluminum foil. Combine brown sugar and spices; rub over ribs, turning to coat evenly.

Bring up foil sides. Double-fold top and one end to seal packet. Through open end, add ¼ cup water or 3 to 4 ice cubes. Double-fold open end, leaving room for heat circulation inside. Repeat to make 2 packets

Grill 45 to 60 minutes in covered grill, then remove ribs from foil and place on grill.

Brush ribs with barbecue sauce. Continue grilling 10 to 15 minutes, brushing with sauce and turning every 5 minutes.

Herbed Vegetable Packet

Pat Schweitzer and Betty Morton/Reprinted from *Pat and Betty's No-Fuss Cooking* (Hyperion)

Serves 6

This straightforward recipe is healthy and delicious, and can be adjusted to incorporate any your favorite vegetables. Be sure to cut the vegetables uniformly, so they cook evenly.

1 sheet (18 by 24 inches) Reynolds Wrap® Heavy Duty Aluminum Foil
4 cups broccoli florets
1½ cups peeled baby carrots
1 medium yellow squash, sliced
1 small onion, thinly sliced
1 teaspoon dried basil
1 teaspoon garlic salt
2 tablespoons butter or margarine, cut in pieces
2 ice cubes

Preheat oven to 450 degrees F or grill to medium-high.

Center vegetables on sheet of aluminum foil. Sprinkle with seasonings. Top with butter and ice cubes.

Bring up foil sides. Double-fold top and ends to seal, making one large foil packet. Leave room for heat circulation inside.

Bake 20 to 25 minutes on a cookie sheet in oven, or grill 12 to 16 minutes in covered grill.

Cheesy Chicken Nachos

Pat Schweitzer and Betty Morton/Reprinted from *Pat and Betty's No-Fuss Cooking* (Hyperion)

Serves 6 to 8

You can build upon this basic recipe to suit your taste. Substitute beef, pork, or vegetables.
Add bell peppers or jalapeños. Kids will love customizing their own creations.

**Reynolds Wrap® Release® Non-stick Aluminum
   Foil**
4 cups (about 4 ounces) tortilla chips
2 cups Mexican style shredded cheese, divided
1 cup cooked, shredded chicken
1 cup salsa
1 small tomato, chopped
½ cup sliced black olives
2 green onions, sliced

Preheat oven to 400 degrees F, or grill to medium-high indirect heat. For indirect heat, place food on opposite side of grill, away from heat source, with no coals or flame underneath.

Line a 9 by 13 by 2-inch baking pan with the non-stick aluminum foil, with non-stick side up to hold food. Place tortilla chips in foil-lined pan in an even layer. Sprinkle 1¾ cups cheese over chips.

In a bowl, combine chicken and salsa. Spread over tortilla chips. Top with tomato, black olives, and green onions. Sprinkle with remaining cheese.

Bake 8 to 10 minutes, or grill 5 to 7 minutes, until cheese melts.

Reynolds Kitchens Tip: To line pans with Release® foil, flip pan upside down. Press a sheet of foil around pan with non-stick (dull) side down. Remove foil, maintaining shape. Flip pan upright and drop foil inside with non-stick side facing up. Crimp edges to rim of pan.

To make a foil grill pan, stack two sheets of foil as above, and shape around pan as directed. Remove from pan and crimp top of edges. Place on a tray for support when transporting to and from the grill.

ACKNOWLEDGEMENTS

We'd like first to thank the many talented cookbook authors who appeared on the *Seasonings* programs and contributed their delicious recipes to this cookbook. Big kudos to our host **Dede Wilson**, a highly talented cookbook author and writer herself whose boundless energy and enthusiasm made the shows sparkle.

A huge thank you goes to **KitchenAid**, sponsor of the *Seasonings* series. KitchenAid's commitment is not only to provide home cooks with the best possible kitchen equipment, but also to give them the cooking skills and recipes that will help them make great food. We are especially grateful to Brian Maynard, whose leadership and vision were instrumental in putting this project together, and to Julie Bizzis, whose contributions and support were invaluable. We also thank Justin Newby for his advice and guidance.

A number of companies generously supported our efforts by providing props for the filming and photography, including Wood-Mode, Avonite, Villeroy & Boch, Pfaltzgraff, Mikasa, and Beaulieu Vineyard. Our grateful acknowledgements go to these companies.

And finally, heartfelt thanks to our production staff and crew, whose dedicated hard work maintained such high standards for the look and sound of each show: George Colmer, Colleen Corley, Todd Gardiner, Nathanial Higgs, Rick Kyle, John Reynolds, Deanna Sison, Kathy Tobin, and Gordon Winiemko; and to our dedicated and hard-working kitchen prep cooks, Frederic Desbiens, John Heaman, and Greg Severn.

Marjorie Poore
Alec Fatalevich
Producers